STARTING WITH NIETZSCHE

Continuum's *Starting with . . .* series offers clear, concise and accessible introductions to the key thinkers in philosophy. The books explore and illuminate the roots of each philosopher's work and ideas, leading readers to a thorough understanding of the key influences and philosophical foundations from which his or her thought developed. Ideal for first-year students starting out in philosophy, the series will serve as the perfect companion to study of this fascinating subject.

Available now:

Starting with Derrida, Sean Gaston

Forthcoming in 2009:

Starting with Berkeley, Nick Jones

Starting with Descartes, C.G. Prado

Starting with Hegel, Craid B. Matarrese

Starting with Heidegger, Thomas Greaves

Starting with Hobbes, George Macdonald Ross

Starting with Hume, Charlotte R. Brown and William Edward Morris

Starting with Kant, Andrew Ward

Starting with Leibniz, Lloyd Strickland

Starting with Mill, John R. Fitzpatrick

Starting with Rousseau, James Delaney

Starting with Wittgenstein, Chon Tejedor

STARTING WITH NIETZSCHE

ULLRICH HAASE

continuum

Continuum International Publishing Group
The Tower Building   80 Maiden Lane
11 York Road   Suite 704
London SE1 7NX   New York, NY 10038

www.continuumbooks.com

British Library Cataloguing-in-Publication Data
A catalogue record for this book is available from the British Library.

ISBN: HB: 1–8470–6162–1
978–1–8470–6162–1
PB: 1–8470–6163–X
978–1–8470–6163–8

Library of Congress Cataloging-in-Publication Data
Haase, Ullrich M., 1962–
Starting with Nietzsche / Ullrich Haase.
p. cm.
Includes bibliographical references (p.   ).
ISBN 978–1–84706–162–1 – ISBN 978–1–84706–163–8
1. Nietzsche, Friedrich Wilhelm, 1844–1900.   I. Title.

B3317.H224 2008
193–dc22

2008020303

Typeset by RefineCatch Limited, Bungay, Suffolk
Printed and bound in Great Britain by
MPG Books Ltd, Bodmin, Cornwall

CONTENTS

ABBREVIATIONS

GM	*On the Genealogy of Morality*, Cambridge: Cambridge University Press 1994.
GS	*The Gay Science*, New York: Vintage Books 1974.
HAH	*Human, All too Human*, Cambridge: Cambridge University Press 1996.
HL	*On the Advantage and Disadvantage of History for Life*, Indianapolis & Cambridge: Hackett 1980.
TI	*Twilight of the Idols*, Oxford: Oxford University Press 1998.
TL	'On Truth and Lying in a Non-Moral Sense', from *The Birth of Tragedy and other Writings*, Cambridge: Cambridge University Press 1999, pp. 139–153.
WP	*The Will to Power*, New York: Random House 1973, referenced by section numbers.
Z	*Thus Spake Zarathustra*, London: Penguin Books 1969.

OTHER TEXTS CITED

Decline	Oswald Spengler, *The Decline of the West*, Oxford: Oxford University Press 2007.
Discourse	Gottfried Wilhelm Leibniz, *Discourse on Metaphysics*, Chicago: Open Court 1993.
Eye	Maurice Merleau-Ponty, 'Eye and Mind', in Galen Johnson, ed., *The Merleau-Ponty Aesthetics Reader*, Evanston, IL: Northwestern University Press 1993.
Freedom	Friedrich Wilhelm Joseph Schelling, *Philosophical Inquiries into the Nature of Human Freedom*, Chicago: Open Court 1936.
History	Ralph Waldo Emerson, *Collected Works of Ralph Waldo Emerson: Essays, First Series v. 2*, Cambridge, MA: Harvard University Press 1990.
Jacques	Denis Diderot, *Jacques the Fatalist*, Oxford: Oxford Paperbacks 1999.
Prolegomena	Immanuel Kant, *Prolegomena to any Future*

Metaphysics that can Qualify as a Science, Chicago: Open Court 1994.

PoS   Georg Wilhelm Friedrich Hegel, *Phenomenology of Spirit*, Oxford: Oxford University Press 1977.

INTRODUCTION

O Man! Attend!
What does deep midnight's voice contend?
'I slept my sleep,
'And now awake at dreaming's end:
'The world is deep,
'Deeper than day can comprehend,
'Deep is its woe,
'Joy – deeper than heart's agony:
'Woe says: Fade! Go!
'But all joy wants eternity,
'Wants deep, deep, deep eternity'

The author of these lines is Friedrich Nietzsche (1844–1900), and they can be found, in three different places, in what Nietzsche himself calls the deepest book ever bequeathed to mankind: *Thus Spake Zarathustra*. Most commentaries on Nietzsche's work leave the *Zarathustra* in the background, as it is a rather unusual work, not only in its content but also in its style, and therefore rather difficult to address. It is often the horizon for the understanding of Nietzsche's other works, and it is for this reason that I am going to make use of these lines in order to introduce his philosophical thinking. Nietzsche refers to these lines as a song. This song is called the '*Roundelay*', its name is 'once again' and its meaning is 'in all eternity'. This is the song of the 'Higher Men', of those who are trying to overcome the limitations of 'modern man'.

Nietzsche, more than any other thinker in the history of European philosophy, *is* his work. He dedicated his life from his teens onwards to the development of his philosophy. With this aim in mind he gave up on anything else that life might offer but which could interfere with his work, whether this was love, companionship or earthly possessions. But who is this Friedrich Nietzsche, and how is he still able to speak to us, considering that he speaks from another world, a world preceding the explosions of two world wars and the frantic developments of modern industry and technology, which during the last century, have changed our world beyond recognition?

i. O MAN! ATTEND!

If there is one thing that Nietzsche fought for during his entire life, then it was the attention of his contemporaries. Yet not for the attention to Nietzsche himself. Rather, what he wanted us to attend to is the distress of our age, the distress of an age which deems itself happy. While his contemporaries seemed mostly convinced that the development of science and the advancement of technology would turn the twentieth century into an age of wealth and happiness, Nietzsche was one of the few who realized that all this enthusiasm would issue into wars of a scale the world had never seen before, and into a destruction never intimated in the worst nightmares of the nineteenth century. In nineteenth-century thought, the idea of progress had become inevitable. While the Enlightenment of the seventeenth and eighteenth centuries was building its hope on the idea of a universal reason, on the equality of all human beings given in rational judgement, and therefore, on the goodwill of everyone, the positivism of the natural sciences and the historicism of the human sciences in the nineteenth century got rid of even this requirement of all human beings to agree, in that it based its notion of progress on objective fact. In other words, not even hope was needed to make the world a better place.

That life would by necessity have to turn out for the better also had something to do with the fact that it was not that good in the nineteenth century. The enthusiasm of the French Revolution, issuing in the Napoleonic wars, had not achieved what it set out to do. Instead of liberating European mankind from exploitation and slavery, the beginning of the Industrial Revolution had led to suffering on a scale not known before. But while the idealism of the early nineteenth century did not seem to bear the fruits that it promised, there appeared a materialism which seemed to have broken more radically with the Christian past. In the philosophy of Karl Marx and the positivism of the nineteenth century, the feeling prevailed that where the French Revolution had failed, scientific progress would deliver. Instead this age was followed not only by two world wars, but even more so by the Cold War, that is, the determination of peace as war with other means, as cultural war or science war, as technological war and electronic war, as total mobilization of nation states who endeavour to enlist every single individual in their workforce in order to win the total economic war, even if sometimes under the banner of global cooperation. And it led to the Holocaust, to the industrialized production of death, whose significance is, according to the German philosopher Theodor Adorno, an injunction against poetry. Poetry seems to paint the world in idealistic colours, while after Auschwitz such colours could at best mock the desolate state of the human world.

Are we, then, today in agreement with Nietzsche concerning the problem which he calls *European Nihilism*? No. Somehow we have returned to the spirit of the late nineteenth century, having added the idea of prosperity to it. That is to say, we often think we have found the remedy to the ills of the past, a remedy through which European society will be delivered over into prosperity, wealth and independence from nature. And again it is the idea of the rational sciences that is going to deliver us. We often tend again to attribute all ills of the world to something we vaguely call the 'irrational' and thus put all our hopes on the 'hard' sciences, whether these belong to the biotechnical or the economic installations of our age. Religious sentiment, human judgement, moral convictions, subjective intuition, artistic creation – all these lie on the side of error, so that we often tend to agree that only 'objective' criteria can deliver justice in whatever question is at stake.

Nietzsche would not have been too surprised about any of this. He often called himself the philosopher of the next two centuries, insofar as he knew that history is not changed that easily, especially not if everyone seems to be quite happy with how things are going. Sometimes Nietzsche might have felt like the only passenger on the *Titanic* who knew that something untoward was to happen, and who could have saved the ship if he could just have made people listen. A similar image is given in one fragment from *The Gay Science*, in which the 'madman', i.e. the one not belonging to the crowd, runs into the market square to warn everyone of the world-shattering upheavals which will accompany the *Death of God*. But having screamed 'God is Dead', he is laughed at and vilified, as nobody can see the problem. The *Death of God*, as Nietzsche shows, is not 'only' the disappearance of one 'thing' from amongst all other things, so that these latter would still be left intact; it is also the loss of our faith in the effective power of thinking, so that the people in the market square 'believe' that all they have lost is a 'belief', which is to say, nothing at all.

Attending to the challenges of our age is thus hampered by our not being aware of any problem. Nietzsche responds to this by the idea of the philosopher not as a prophet, who can see things others cannot, but as a physician, who sees the diagnosis and then the acceptance of an illness as the first step on the path towards healing. European nihilism, this illness which we, according to Nietzsche, suffer from, is thus something we would first have to accept as the reality of our age. As Nietzsche says, he is certainly one of the great nihilists of the nineteenth century, but his aim is to defeat this nihilism in order to return to 'some-thing'. This hope of a return – which will not profit *Herrn Nietzsche* himself, given that he just said that it would take at least 200 years before his thinking could have any effect – this hope and meaning of the earth Nietzsche calls the *Übermensch*, sometimes translated as *Superman*, while literally meaning *Overhuman*.

But during his life Nietzsche was never very successful in becoming famous. While his first book, *The Birth of Tragedy from the Spirit of Music*, was read widely, at least in academic circles, with a few hundred copies sold; while the fourth untimely meditation, *Wagner in Bayreuth*, was at least widely read in the circle of the Wagner Societies, most of the other works were practically ignored. The fourth part of the *Zarathustra* was only printed for private circulation, while many other books – *Beyond Good and Evil*, *On the Genealogy of Morality*, *The Case of Wagner*, *The Twilight of the Idols* and *The Antichrist* – were printed at Nietzsche's own expense. Nietzsche suffered throughout the 1880s from this ignorance of his work and from his intolerable loneliness. The analogy with the physician might help again. Here a realization of the illness is required for there to be any chance of healing, and yet there is no time to be lost. Nietzsche's thought, then, the teaching of the *Eternal Return of the Same*, of *Overhuman* or *Will to Power*, is designed to make this realization possible, to bring about a crisis in the existence of humankind. Nietzsche calls himself a destiny, dynamite, the one who will break European history into two.

Nietzsche had spent the 1880s working, working and working. He had been a very serious child, who tried to persuade other children to drop their toys for the sake of literary discourse, and later he tried to persuade his fellow students to forgo the beer and engage in academic discourse. In the early 1880s he gave up his position as a professor at the University of Basel, Switzerland, in order to dedicate the rest of his life to his work. Being of rather frail health, he spent the last years of the 1880s travelling back and forth between Nice, on the Côte d'Azur, where he passed his winters, and the Oberengadin, the highest plateau of Europe, in south-east Switzerland, mainly so as to keep the temperature and humidity stable throughout the year. *Herr Nietzsche* is his work: he is this dynamite and nothing else. There is no such division here as 'the man and the thinker', even though the various masks that the author is wearing in his books seem to demand of the reader to uncover the true Nietzsche underneath. Being his work, Nietzsche comes more and more to depend on it.

> I live on my own credit, it is perhaps merely a prejudice that I am alive at all? . . . I need only to talk with any of the 'cultured people' who come to the Ober-Engadin in the summer to convince myself that I am *not* alive . . . Under these circumstances there exists a duty, . . . namely to say: *Listen to me! for I am thus and thus. Do not, above all, confound me with what I am not!* (EH 3)

At the end of the 1880s Nietzsche lost his patience more and more. Something had to be done to resolve the problems of Europe. Insofar as its problems were on the political level, with the various nation states waging war against each other, Nietzsche was the first convinced European. When he speaks of Napoleon having been responsible for the only recent reasons for any hope, he refers to the latter's aim to unify Europe, thereby putting an end to the particular national interests and to the history of monarchies dividing Europe according to their private interests. Racism and nationalism are, Nietzsche argues, outmoded conceptions missing the reality of a common European heritage. Something had to be done and, with the onset of his nervous breakdown, Nietzsche wrote letters to the

Emperors of Germany and Italy and to Bismarck, the 'Iron Chancellor' of Germany. He tried to persuade them to attend a summit on the future of Europe. At the same time he wrote to friends, unveiling his plan to lure these three into a meeting where he would, as they were the main bulwarks against European unity, shoot them. These notes belong to what are often referred to as his 'madness notes' and yet, mad as they might be, they are also relentlessly logical.

ii. WHAT DOES DEEP MIDNIGHT'S VOICE CONTEND?

We are then not to pay attention to Nietzsche's private opinions, but to those questions to which he dedicated his life. These can be summed up by the question: 'What remains of the human world after the *Death of God*?' 'God': that was the name for the natural light of reason allowing for an understanding of the world. We have already heard about the Enlightenment, spanning from the famous French philosopher René Descartes to the German thinker Immanuel Kant. This Enlightenment was deeply Christian. It promised a progressive mastery of the world precisely by the divine gift of reason. It was therefore also the time of the conception and birth of the natural sciences. The promise of this Enlightenment then depends on the universality and hence indubitability of the laws of reason and its mathematical structure. For that to be possible, Descartes had already argued that mind and body are two different substances. The mind or soul is the locus of freedom and understanding, of a light shed onto the world. The body, on the other hand, is characterized by its mechanical, causal nature. Consequently the Enlightenment elaborates its promise of progress through the idea that the rational mind has to master the irrational emotions. Light has to banish the shadows. Why then should we attend to the voice of the 'deep midnight'?

Nietzsche is often credited as a precursor of psychoanalysis, insofar as the voice of midnight seems to refer to something like the unconscious, and has been taken up especially in the artistic movements of the early twentieth century. But Nietzsche has more in mind here. The Enlightenment has flattened our understanding of the world to mere surface phenomena. Rather than being able to understand the whole world, it reduces the world to that which can be understood. As Nietzsche once said, it prefers a few drab facts to whole wagonloads of beautiful possibilities. This is also why it can be so blind as to the modern condition. The Enlightenment hence ignores the two main realities of the human world: that is, the body and history, both of which cannot be reduced to the presence of facts. 'I know what is shadow and what light: what is body and what soul – on this you are not very bright' (8/401), Nietzsche says, thereby contending that we have misunderstood up to now the very notion of the understanding.

iii. I SLEPT MY SLEEP, AND NOW AWAKE AT DREAMING'S END

Nietzsche understands European history – that is, the history of philosophy ending in the formulation of the modern natural sciences – as a dream. To do so is the general movement of scepticism, asking of what knowledge we can be sure that it really relates to a world independent from our mind. And yet Nietzsche is not an idealist who would claim that, finally, every truth that is relevant to us is only a function of the mind. Rather he calls this a dream, because a dream is a production of images which are only mediately related to the real. But insofar as philosophy has understood the idea of thinking itself through its separation from the world of appearances, Nietzsche can say that the whole of metaphysics, of philosophy since Plato, has been a dream. This does not mean that it was wrong, in as much as all historical creation is an artistic creation and hence semblance, which is to say, make-believe. The problem is rather that today's philosophy is a dream in which one can no longer believe, a dream that forces us to wake up. And this waking up takes the form of a confrontation with nihilism.

But are the modern scientists not already claiming that science equally concerns a waking up from the idealistic dreams of theology? A waking up that shows the errors of the true world and delivers us over to the naked world of scientific fact? A waking up that moves us, against our will, from dreaming of being sons and daughters of God towards the reality that we are but sons and daughters of apes? And that, as such sons and daughters, all ideas of freedom and political self-determination were but sweet dreams? God is dead and, consequently, we have to abolish the 'true world', that is, the world that exists in a true sense, insofar as within it nothing ever changes: that world, therefore, which guaranteed that we ourselves could transcend the life of animals. Which world is left? The world of the natural sciences. A world of pure fact, without consolation, without solace. A world in which pride exists because the world can be known, and yet this known world is a world in which nothing is of any consequence, as it is a world without meaning. And yet, this world is known from the perspective of a neutral, objective consciousness; it is known by a knowledge which is not a part of it. But that is to say, with Nietzsche, that it is this world which is a dream, that 'with the true world we have also abolished the apparent world'. Nietzsche's philosophy of suspicion is thus not primarily turned against the Christian faith in opposition to the rationality of the sciences, but against this idea of rationality as such.

> My writings have been called a schooling in suspicion, even more in contempt, but fortunately also in courage, indeed in audacity. And in fact I myself do not believe that anyone has ever before looked into the world with an equally profound degree of suspicion, and not only as an occasional devil's advocate, but, to speak theologically, just as much as an enemy and indicter of God. (HAH 5)

But how was it possible to forget the world of the body and history? How was it possible to make philosophy an abstract thinking of that which is visible, of pure fact? Because we tend to overlook that which is closest to us. For thousands of years philosophers have asked questions about the reality of truth, about the being of God, about freedom and immortality, while that which is closest to them, the everyday life of the human being, seemed to have vanished. We have thus forgotten the night on which every day depends; we have privileged memory to the detriment of forgetting. 'What everyone knows is forgotten by everyone; and if there was no night, nobody would be able to know what light is!' (10/415).

iv. THE WORLD IS DEEP, DEEPER THAN DAY CAN COMPREHEND

The day of understanding thus only skims the surface of reality. What it calls truth is a surface phenomenon, a dream of the soul pretending to be all reality. But with the *Death of God*, we no longer have a right to the soul. What we find in its stead, the body, delivers us over to a historical world much deeper than the daylight of reason can fathom. Here the pride of the understanding is humbled and many questions present themselves only in the form of riddles. Sometimes Nietzsche makes these points quite forcefully, ridiculing the superficial, objective world of the Enlightenment. 'We disdain everything that can be explained. Some stupidity has had herself surprised and now stands naked in front of her explainer' (10/415).

It is this discovery of the depth of the life-world that is so exciting in the reading of Nietzsche's text. And to begin with, reading Nietzsche should be an exhilarating experience, even though often accompanied with challenges, some of them unpleasant, to one's general beliefs and convictions. Nietzsche's style of writing is compelling, his prose is sparkling, his argumentation is clear and, it seems, immediately accessible. Instead of a complicated argument trying to establish whether nine or twelve categories might govern the use of human understanding, Nietzsche philosophizes, as he says himself, with a hammer. The reader is presented with a wealth of ideas, with piercing perceptions on the part of a sharp intellect, which combines metaphysical and psychological insights with reflections on the essential history of art, morality and the culture of European humankind from the age of Heraclitus and Plato to our days. And these insights are coupled with a wealth of new conceptions, which exert a fascination precisely because they are equally suggestive: when Nietzsche speaks of the *Eternal Return of the Same*, of the '*Superman*' or of the *Will to Power*, of the *Death of God* or '*European Nihilism*', each of these has an immediate effect on our experience of the world as it presents itself to us in the twenty-first century.

Thus, initially, most readers of Nietzsche feel very confident that they have acquired a comprehensive grasp of the thoughts presented just by reading his books themselves. What would one need help with in the face of such an immediately clear text, a text which seems weighed down neither by complex terminology, like, for example, Kant's *Critique of Pure Reason*, nor by the twists and turns of the systematic concretion of thought exhibited, for example, by Hegel's *Phenomenology of Spirit*? When dealing with these two latter books it is clear that one needs a teacher to be able to understand their overall motivation, let alone any particular argument, whereas Nietzsche's work presents itself as eminently readable.

And yet, if this really was the case, would that not mean that, besides not needing any help in understanding Nietzsche, we would not learn much from Nietzsche either, and all his text would be able to do is reconfirm our innermost prejudices? Indeed, there are many readers of Nietzsche who attempt to collect all those phrases that confirm their own prejudices and who, subsequently, attempt to discount all those which do not. Having done so, their hands are as empty as they were before reading Nietzsche.

Maybe one of the main reasons for this unbearable lightness of interpretation is based upon the mistaking of the unsystematic structure of Nietzsche's work for a laxity of argument itself. It has often been held that Nietzsche argues that there is no truth and that, therefore, every interpretation is allowed. It has even been suggested that being unsystematic, Nietzsche's work might just mean anything to anyone. Analytic philosophers often claim that what they call 'Continental Philosophy' lacks in rigour and clarity of argument. And yet, Nietzsche's thinking follows a much more rigorous argumentation than one built on adherence to rules of formal logic. It is built on philological method and, finally, on what Nietzsche frequently refers to as 'our honesty'. Instead of 'applying' established rules of thinking to the world, hoping that they might find something in there, Nietzsche understands philosophy as the 'voluntary life in ice and high mountains – the seeking out of all that which is foreign and question-worthy in existence . . .' (6/158).

The apparent ease of reading Nietzsche's works partly accounts for the fact that he is, without doubt, the most widely read thinker since the beginning of philosophy in the fourth century BC. Nietzsche is read not only by academic philosophers but by academics from many different subject areas. And he is read not only by academics, but by people from all walks of life. His works are used in a wide variety of ways, from quotation collections for managers to critical reflections on the part of teenagers in revolt. He has been used by left-wing interpreters of the generation of the 1968 student revolts as much as by the Nazis, who tried to install him as their leading light. In response to that latter use, the German philosopher Martin Heidegger gave lectures on Nietzsche from 1936 to 1942, which have been called the only intellectual resistance against the Nazi regime from within Germany. Nietzsche is seen as the destroyer of the Christian faith, while at the same time providing inspiration to contemporary Protestant theology.

Obviously, this interest does not rely merely on the fact that Nietzsche's language is accessible and persuasive. He rather seems to 'hit a nerve'; he seems to say something that appeals to our need to understand ourselves and the world we live in. Speaking at the same time in a contemporary register and with a view to the beginnings of European philosophy in ancient Greece, Nietzsche is able to speak to us from the vantage point of our historical essence. And he has an ability to speak to us in a way that can, depending on the ability to listen, have a radically liberating effect. Consider this witness statement by the influential twentieth-century French philosopher Michel Foucault:

> Nietzsche was a revelation to me. I felt that there was something quite different from what I had been taught. I read him with a great passion and broke with my life, left my job in the asylum, left France: I had the feeling I had been trapped. Through Nietzsche I became a stranger to all that.

Not every reader of Nietzsche has experienced such an effect and not everyone shares the same understanding of his works. Instead, invited into his work by its open structure and style, many readers lose themselves within the vast reaches of his work, which often refuses to give a helping hand to its readers. That is to say, there is no work of Nietzsche which one could understand as laying the foundation of a system that could progressively be conquered by the understanding. Equally, his works are not structured according to the various topics that one might want to understand within the boundaries of philosophy. Thus whether one wants to know about Nietzsche's ideas about art or politics, about history, morality or religion, there is no proper signposting to guide the reader through his works.

Even worse, individual texts often seem contradictory to the extent that a reader loses any idea of what Nietzsche might have believed or not. In the same work, and only separated by a few pages, the reader can find sentences like 'there is no such thing as the will' and 'everything is will against will'. If the reader finally manages to make her way to *Thus Spake Zarathustra*, she is confronted with a text which does not give up its secrets without a fight. There are hardly any straightforward sentences in this work and it is not even clear what kind of book one has in one's hands. A novel? A book of philosophy? Or neither? And if a book of philosophy, why does Nietzsche never just speak his mind?

So why does Nietzsche often refuse to guide the reader through his texts? As we will see, the notion of philosophical thinking as well as that of human understanding generally forbid Nietzsche to make understanding easy. The philosopher's task is to move his readers, but for such motion to be possible there needs to be resistance. As Nietzsche once said about the *Zarathustra*, anyone who has not felt outrage against every sentence in it has not really understood it. This is not because Nietzsche wants to shock us. In opposition to first impressions, Nietzsche is a rather 'untimely' thinker. His truths are going so much against the grain of modern man, of our enlightenment beliefs, that anyone who feels herself merely confirmed by Nietzsche's writings cannot have understood them. It is akin to the image that Plato gives in the allegory of the cave, the founding myth of all philosophy: insofar as philosophical liberation has to force us to cut through the chains of habit, it has to hurt.

The initial openness of Nietzsche's work thus all too soon shows itself to be a lure. Nietzsche speaks of himself as a fisherman who throws out his net in order to catch himself some readers. These enter his texts without much difficulty, but in order for there to be any essential effect of these works, these readers will have to struggle to get out again. They can either get out by reducing the text to indifferent beliefs, which they might share or not, or they will leave it by having been changed essentially, so that they cannot again be caught in such nets.

In this introduction, I shall not claim to be able to present a road map or even an autopilot leading the reader through Nietzsche's texts without loss of comfort. Instead, all I will try to do is to give some indication as to how one might be *Starting with Nietzsche*. As the modern theory of interpretation tells us, everything depends on the prejudices that one brings to a work. These prejudices can be partly negated or affirmed in the process of reading. Thus, for example, to approach the reading of Nietzsche's text having heard before that Nazi Germany attempted to install Nietzsche as its lodestar, will influence the understanding one gains concerning the idea of the *Superman*, or, literally translated, the *Overhuman*.

In this sense, everything depends on how one starts with reading Nietzsche. But, much more importantly than being influenced, positively or negatively, concerning certain ideas prominently featuring in Nietzsche's work, what is even more decisive is that one should be careful about what idea of philosophy itself one pre-supposes when picking up a text. What is philosophy? What does a philosopher try to do when writing a text? What can one expect from philosophy? These are questions to which we often have an implicit answer and this answer, however unreflected it might be, forms the foundation of our understanding of the work we read.

v. DEEP IS ITS WOE

We have already encountered the idea of European history as the history of nihilism. But it is not the case that Nietzsche here sees a fault with, for example, Plato's thinking. Nietzsche's first book is called *The Birth of Tragedy from the Spirit of Music*. As he says himself of this book, it first of all brought the problem of the modern sciences into our perspective. Reading about the transition from the 'tragic world view' of classical Greece to the beginnings of philosophy, one might equally have called this book *The Birth of Philosophy from the Spirit of Tragedy*. Nietzsche describes the tragic age of the Greeks as a pessimism of strength. This encapsulates the idea that, accepting the limitations of life and its sufferings, the Greeks could have affirmed just about any world, not just the best of all possible worlds.

With the Platonic–Christian interpretation of life, on the other hand, suffering became more and more an argument against life. Life itself was progressively seen as an illness which could not be healed except by death. To affirm life was only possible from the perspective of its end. Death hence becomes the great liberator, the great and only hope for a deliverance from suffering. It is from here that Christianity has become the religion of pity. Consequently, Nietzsche argues that Christianity paves the way for a 'slave moral-ity', which is to say, an interpretation of human existence from the perspective of those who suffer life and suffer from life. Life thus comes to be interpreted from the perspective of its opposite, that is, from the non-perspective of universal reason. This is supposed to heal us from suffering. But 'our intellect has not been made for the conception of becoming' (9/500), and what it takes to be a medica-tion for the good thus turns out to be the greatest poison ever invented.

vi. JOY – DEEPER THAN HEART'S AGONY; WOE SAYS: FADE! GO!

What then is the task of philosophy? For Nietzsche, the value of thought, indeed the value of anything, is, in the last analysis, to be led back to the perspective of life. 'Does it further life or does it stultify life?' is the question to be posed to any thought and any human action. As we will see, this is not a superficial approach to philosophy, neither does it point a naïve happiness as the aim of all human beings. Instead, it needs an understanding of the most contradictory and tortured sides of human action and emotion to understand its various endeavours. Looking at all that the European human being has done over the last 2,500 years, from wars to artistic creation, from empires and their organization to the building of universities and the development of the modern, mathematical sciences; whatever it may be, finally it is a question of its value for life. This 'philosophy of life' characterizes Nietzsche's thinking from early on and it is for this reason that he affirmatively quotes the German poet Hölderlin, who said that 'he who has wondered about the most profound things, loves that which is most alive' (7/711). It is here that a topic appears that has led to a lot of misunderstanding. As Nietzsche says, the philosopher of the future has to be an advocate of suffering. However, this is not to say that she should seek out suffering or even increase it, but it is to counter the devaluation of life on account of Christianity, for which, as Nietzsche says, suffering counts as an argument against life.

Against this nihilism of modernity, against this life which suffers from life, there are no good arguments. There is only the hope of being able to destroy its values and to re-evaluate them. As Nietzsche belongs to this world, the destruction cannot be done from the outside: nihilism can thus only be destroyed by an even more radical nihilism. The problem for such a philosophical undertaking is something Nietzsche had already realized as a teenager, when composing an essay on 'Fate and History', in which he writes: 'I have tried to deny everything: oh, to tear down is easy, but to build! And even tearing down appears easier than it actually is' (BAW 2/55). That tearing down appears easier than it actually is, is a truth that haunted Nietzsche from the moment he wrote these words. That to build is even harder is something which finally broke him. From 1884 onwards, Nietzsche proceeds to write his magnum opus, a positive work of philosophy, re-evaluating all values that have informed Christian existence. There are many plans and thousands of pages of notes outlining the various ideas concerning this work. On some plans appears the title 'The Antichrist' as an introduction, a last use of the hammer in philosophizing, as an overture to the great philosophy that is to come. Finally it is only this introduction that is to appear, being written in the last year of his self-conscious existence; that is to say, in 1888.

To find that joy, deeper than heart's agony, which could express itself in philosophical thinking is something that Nietzsche never quite achieved but to which he came closest in the development of the no-longer-philosopher, Zarathustra. And yet Nietzsche was never naïvely thinking that the aim of life could be to recreate itself spontaneously. Not even Zarathustra is a 'superman' or an *Overhuman*, but he is the one who can claim to be the teacher of the *Eternal Return of the Same* and of the *Overhuman*, which is to say that he can affirm life as the 'forefather' of he who might one day redeem existence. But is existence really that bad? Do we really suffer that much? With Nietzsche we have to bear in mind that he speaks about 'essential suffering'. While we can be well fed or even rich, content with our lives and our social existence, these do not bring satisfaction. They characterize a lack of certain pains, but no human fulfilment. The analysis of the *Will to Power* shows for Nietzsche that all willing is essentially a willing beyond oneself, a will to self-overcoming. While Freud later wrote that the human being is the battleground of the fight between Eros and Thanatos, between love and the 'death drive', for Nietzsche the *Will to Power* shows itself as being both in one, indistinguishably Dionysos. And yet, today, we can no longer project our will into the future; we are incapable of valuing anything that is not present: 'the world is all that is the case', as another philosopher from the twentieth century, Wittgenstein, has said. The thought of the *Eternal Return of the Same* is thus to bring this crisis to a decisive point, to bring it out in all its reality. This crisis, this decision is that between animal and *Overhuman*.

Nietzsche sees his own thought within a moment of crisis in the existence of the human being. He understands his thought as a doctrine, that is, a teaching, which moves the reader from here to there, from sickness to health. Equally, thus, the reading of such a philosophy should be a transition. When Nietzsche finally found a reader of his work in the Danish philosopher Georg Brandes, he wrote to him: 'It was no great feat to find me, considering that you had already discovered me: the difficulty now is to lose me again'.

vii. BUT ALL JOY WANTS ETERNITY, WANTS DEEP, DEEP, DEEP ETERNITY

Joy is the expression of the will in its highest affirmation, and it is this joy which rises above heart's agony – that is, above a passive suffering of life. But somehow the will can affirm itself only in self-overcoming and it is for this reason that it has always desired eternity. Since Plato, human life is possible insofar as the human being tries to claim for itself the pleasures of the gods, that is, the possibility of immortality. But, since God is dead, it seems that this hope of justifying existence by way of looking towards the gods has finally left us. Human life is that life which cannot live without truth; all truth appears as an aspiration to the absolute. The idea of an eternity, transcending the ephemeral nature of the present, thus seems to be necessary to human life. And yet, the infinite also threatens what is affirmed by it. What if life has to be affirmed by something beyond life and there is no longer any beyond? An affirmation that reaches beyond oneself one might call a longing for this beyond. This longing Nietzsche calls understanding the *Overhuman* as the meaning of this earth. Such understanding can be reached only in an account of the teaching of the *Eternal Return of the Same*. 'Do you understand my longing, my longing for the finite? The longing of him who has seen the ring of recurrence?' (11/226)

During autumn and winter of the year 1888 Nietzsche takes up residence in Turin. Everything is perfect and beautiful. He writes obsessively, he sends letters full of praise about Turin, its inhabitants, about the prices and the beauties, about his abundant health. He is convinced that he has never been as strong and healthy as now; he is convinced that his best years are still lying ahead. On the third day of January 1889, Nietzsche witnesses a man beating his horse. Moved by pity he goes to the horse's rescue, embraces it, and proves with his ensuing madness that pity is a vice. The last eleven years of his life he spends in various institutions and looked after first by his mother, then by his sister. Most of his waking days he plays the piano.

CHAPTER 1

PHILOSOPHY AS LOVE OF FATE

. . . your educators cannot be anything else but your liberators. And this is the secret of all education. . . . it is a liberation, a clearing away of all weeds, debris, of worms which threaten to taste the tender seeds of plants, emanation of light and warmth, the loving fall of rain at night, it is emulation and adoration of nature . . . (1/341)

What is philosophy? We too easily take it for granted that the task of philosophy is to represent the true state of the world by means of positive, affirmative judgements. These are positive, insofar as one says what a thing is, rather than what it is not, and they are affirmative in that one silently adds that one does believe in their truth. Thus one says, for example, '[I believe that] water boils at 100° Celsius', thereby saying something true about water. While to extend such an idea to all the various questions of philosophy, whether they be moral, investigating the nature of knowledge or ascertaining the existence of God, seems more difficult, it is still often taken to be the aim of philosophical investigations. These are, then, directed towards establishing indubitable truths, that is, truths about which one could no longer disagree. In other words, one often thinks that the idea of philosophy is to 'get it right', so that the worth of a philosophy would be determined by how much it does get right.

But is this superficially plausible idea of philosophy at all meaningful? What would drive anyone to philosophy, if there were nothing more to do than 'getting it right'? With respect to such an idea of philosophy, the philosopher would not achieve anything but the construction of an edifice of ideas which would then be tested by the degree to which it mirrors reality. While the idea of such an edifice is that it would allow us to understand the world better, it still has two essential flaws: the first is that it would remain completely indifferent to the world that we live in, and thus would have no direct influence on our actions. The second flaw is that in order to test the veracity of such a system of ideas, we have to presuppose that reality is already given to us in a clear and distinct way, which is to say that we have to presuppose that the meaning of reality is given in its pure presence to us; that is, that the world is the sum total of all facts. Such an idea of philosophy thinks of truth in an atemporal, ahistorical sense. The ideas that are thought to represent the world are themselves understood to be non-changing, logical entities. These are deemed to exist independently of the world and they are thought not to be affected by the way the world changes. In other words, they are metaphysical ideas in that they transcend the level of historical change that characterizes the world itself.

Nietzsche claims that all philosophy hitherto was Platonic, in that it separates the world of becoming, i.e. the world in which we live with all our experiences, our thought and our emotions, from the world of being, that is, the world of true essences. We might no longer believe that this true world of ideas actually exists in heaven, and that the things in our world are merely copies of these ideas. We might have given up on the idea of a transmigration of the soul explaining our ability to understand the world, and yet we still believe that the level of truth, as the relation of clear and distinct ideas, is one completely separate from the world of experience. In other words, with respect to the question of truth we might no longer be Platonic realists, but we are still Cartesian idealists, which is to say that we believe that these ideas exist only in the mind, while still retaining the aspect of eternal self-sameness as logical entities. Even when we say in a despairing fashion that 'these are just words', we affirm that they are what they are independent of the world.

While it seems that only Plato really argued for a distinction between a true world of ideas in heaven, and an appearing world, in which we live, we are all Platonic enough to believe what is effectively the same thing, if in different forms. The very idea of reason implies that the reason I give is independent from myself, that is, from my experience, or, indeed, from anybody's experience. For example, the modern theory of genetics is rather Platonic, in that it explicitly excludes the possibility that any actual experience could be genetically transmitted, which means that experience itself has no positive effect on the life of a species. This ideality of reason is the ground on which (a) I can give a rational argument for anything, which is to say that I can argue with somebody, without merely restating my opinions; (b) I can look at history as a well of good or bad ideas; and (c) I can happily make judgements about other people – from other times or other cultures. If the idea I have of a tree, of justice, of friendship, of blue, etc., was not independent from all experience, how should I be able to talk at all? How should I be able to understand anybody except for myself? Modern philosophers have always feared that without this idea of a universal and eternal form of truth, we would get stuck in a relativistic idea of knowledge, to a degree that we could not communicate anything in language; that, ultimately, human language would not be that different from the sounds made by cows or bats.

This problem has often forced philosophers to conclude, explicitly or instinctively and in a rather traditional manner, that philosophy must be a matter of a reasonable conjunction of clear and distinct ideas. If such thought understands itself, furthermore, as systematic, it can be likened to playing with Lego bricks. The philosopher would be in possession of a certain amount of bricks – that is, ideas – which she would fit together into a construction which 'looks like' the world. Thus, when commentators count or discount certain 'ideas' of Nietzsche, like the *Eternal Return of the Same* or the *Will to Power*, they make decisions as to whether this brick in itself corresponds to a fact in the world and as to whether it fits into the overall building constructed of all the bricks that the text makes available. And, if they finally discount the thought of Nietzsche more generally, they make the claim that all these ideas contained in his text do not add up to a proper, fully finished model.

The main problem with the majority of literature on Nietzsche's thought is that it takes this idea of philosophy to be self-evident. Let us take one example, namely Kaufmann's *Nietzsche: Philosopher, Psychologist, Antichrist*. Here Kaufmann discusses the different ways in which Nietzsche's text has been interpreted. Some readers prefer the published works, some the notebooks; some mix early and late texts and others proceed more chronologically. But how does one legitimate one method in view of others? As Kaufmann argues, to give prevalence to the notebooks or even use them with the same emphasis 'seems wholly unjustifiable' (Kaufman 1975, 78). But why and in view of what? The reason is given as revealing Nietzsche's 'final views' (77). There seems then to be a dual interest in a writer. The philosopher evaluates the 'final views' with respect to their coherence and usefulness in the construction of a finished, systematic Lego model, while the philologist or historian of ideas tries to find out how Nietzsche arrived at holding such 'final views'. And once the model is constructed, one can either use it as a 'belief system' or discard the system and use some of the ideas to build another. In any case, such beliefs or views leave us rather indifferent, and a philosophical method that proceeds, to give another image, like a combine harvester to ravage the textual field of Nietzsche studies in order to bring home only the good grains, will never be able to wonder whether it is grain we want.

We will see in more detail why this is not at all Nietzsche's understanding of philosophy; that it is, furthermore, not an idea of philosophy common to most of the great philosophers – and, indeed, that it is not a very meaningful idea of philosophy. Since Plato's 'Allegory of the Cave', philosophy has made it clear that it lies in a war with common sense concerning the understanding of thought. In this allegory Plato has shown the paucity of 'beliefs', 'ideas' or 'views', as we call them nowadays. These 'views' do not relate in any essential sense to ourselves, i.e. they leave us indifferent, and they do not capture the truth of reality.

In another seminal renewal of this antagonism to common sense, Georg Wilhelm Hegel, in the opening chapter of the *Phenomenology of Spirit* (1807), demonstrates the inability to express beliefs, insofar as these are completely abstract and thus find meaning only in personal intention. These *Meinungen* remain mine [*mein*], that is, they cannot be lifted to the level of language, they can thus not be communicated and remain empty words, contradicting each other in their indifference. In a later chapter on scepticism, Hegel describes this sophistry of world views: this 'talk is in fact like the squabbling of self-willed children, one of whom says *A* if the other says *B*, and in turn says *B* if the other says *A*, and who by contradicting *themselves* buy for themselves the pleasure of continually contradicting *one another*' (PoS 126).

The truth of philosophy is found, for Nietzsche, on a completely different level, quite apart from ideas of extreme subjectivity or absolute objectivity – that is, from 'views' held only by me and 'views' that have to be held by everyone – so that it is not even a contradiction to this truth when Nietzsche says, in a letter to a friend: 'my life now consists in the wish that all things might be otherwise than I understand them; and that somebody will come and make my "truths" unbelievable' (KSA-B610). That this wish has not been granted is one of the reasons for which Nietzsche's writings still exert such fascination. Or, as Georg Picht has put it in his brilliant lectures on Nietzsche: 'Why do we read Nietzsche? Because everything he said has become true'. In the following I will try to argue that the doctrines of Nietzsche make sense only if they are seen as actions in the living history of (philosophical) thinking.

i. WHAT IS THE TASK OF PHILOSOPHY?

In order to understand the various doctrines of Nietzsche's philosophy, we have to reflect on the essence of philosophy as he sees it. Once we understand what the task of the Nietzschean philosopher is, the meaning of his philosophy will follow quite straightforwardly. For this to happen, we have to gain an insight into the historical dimension of philosophical thinking, which is to say that we have to realize that philosophy is not just the universal idea of abstract thinking, but essentially grasps the history of European thought from Plato to the present.

Nietzsche is by training a classical philologist. During his school-days he learned to admire the greatness of the Greek age of the artistic human being. His first explicit philosophical influence came from reading the German philosopher Arthur Schopenhauer and, after securing a professorship in classical philology at the University of Basel, Switzerland, he directed his interest more and more towards philosophy. However, this does not constitute a change of interest and, indeed, his fascination with the classical Greek age never subsided, but essentially influenced his philosophical thought. Thus, while he was a brilliant scholar, his interest in the classics was always philosophically motivated.

As he writes in a text from 1874: 'I do not know what meaning classical studies could have for our time if they were not untimely – that is to say, acting counter to our time and thereby acting on our time and, let us hope, for the benefit of a time to come' (HL 8). As you can see, the past does not even get a mention in this passage. According to Nietzsche, it does not make much sense simply to accumulate correct knowledge about events of the past. If thinking about the past makes any sense at all, it is to enlighten our presence and thus to change our future. That is why this text, *On the Advantage and Disadvantage of History for Life*, is opened by a quotation from the German poet Goethe: 'Moreover I hate everything which merely instructs me without increasing or directly quickening my activity'.

It is in this context that Nietzsche says:

> Maybe one will judge in a few centuries' time, that all German philosophizing finds its proper dignity in a progressive rediscovery of the ancient soil, and that all claims to 'originality' sound miserable and laughable with respect to this higher claim of the Germans, namely to have reconnected the bond to the Greeks, ... a bond with the hitherto highest type of human being. (WP 419)

As to this higher type of human being, Nietzsche does not mean to say that all Greeks were artists in our modern sense of the world, but that they saw the whole of life not as the opposition between free human beings and a world of facts, but itself as a work of art.

Many of Nietzsche's early writings are dedicated to understanding this higher type of human being who is not chained to a world of facts. His first book, *The Birth of Tragedy from the Spirit of Music* (1872), is devoted to an investigation into the opposition of the Greek gods Apollo and Dionysos as the Greek deities of the arts. Apollo, as the god of the visual arts, and Dionysos as the god of music, of dream and intoxication, open up the stage of the classic tragic plays as the art form central to the Greek understanding of life. There are many essays and lectures from the same time – 'The Dionysian World-Picture', 'Greek Musical Drama', 'Socrates and Tragedy', 'The Birth of Tragic Thinking' (all from 1870) – and the later, also unpublished but today more famous essays 'Philosophy in the Tragic Age of the Greeks' and 'On Truth and Lying in a Non-Moral Sense' (1873). In order to understand Nietzsche's argument about the Greek as the higher type of human being, we will have a look at 'On Truth and Lying in a Non-Moral Sense'.

The first part of this essay argues for a reversal in the relation between truth and lie. We generally tend to think that there is, first of all, truth pure and simple, while the lie is seen as a question of morality. A lie in this sense is always told on the basis of knowing the truth, while, looking for an advantage in fooling somebody else, we tell a lie. In this sense, truth is a question of facts, and lies belong to the realm of moral considerations. And yet, as Nietzsche demonstrates, the original function of the intellect can only have been one of dissimulation, trickery and entrapment, long before there could ever have been a question of telling the truth. Indeed, it is only with the rise of society that the human being begins to demand a telling of the truth, in order to make members of a given society more reliable. Thus we do not really seek the truth pure and simple, but the agreement of all. It is not difficult to find this point in modern philosophy. Looking at René Descartes, the founder of modern thought, we can see that the notion of certainty does not change anything with respect to our experience of the world or our understanding of things. What it aims at is indubitability, which is to say, a necessity for all to agree. In order to found such truth, one needs to make everybody experience the same, feel the same, think the same, until the world of human beings has been shaped in such a way that nobody could possibly disagree with this newly created universal image of reality.

Nietzsche thus accounts for objectivity as a necessarily communal value, which is to say that it is never free from the exertion of power. If a majority of scientists agree on something, then they have the right and the power to make others agree. If a scientist still refuses to agree, then the majority can, as the twentieth-century logical positivist Rudolf Carnap has argued, say of him that he is colour-blind or a bad observer or fantasizing or a liar or mad (*Erkenntnis* 3/180). That this notion of scientific objectivity directs itself to the necessary agreement of all means for Nietzsche that it does not discover any truths about the world, but works at the normalization of experience. As he says later in the *Zarathustra*, here 'everyone wants the same, everyone is equal to himself: whoever feels differently voluntarily goes to the madhouse' (4/20).

But what do all these points have to do with the question of the task of philosophy? What Nietzsche tries to demonstrate in this essay is that our convictions concerning the notion of truth as certainty of knowledge, this certainty in turn understood as an objectivity of knowledge based in facts, does not ground in itself, but is the consequence of another motivation. Modern philosophers often pride themselves on the scientific nature of their enquiries.

They repudiate, for example, Nietzsche's thought as being 'merely literature', which is to say art. And art they understand as making things appear in a way that they are not. That is, art lies about reality, while, if we are lucky, it lies in an entertaining way. And yet, as Nietzsche has just shown, science, understanding itself as establishing factual truths, belongs to the realm of morality, while the underlying truth of this moral imperative is the lie, that is, an artistic falsification of reality. It is a falsification of reality, making this reality appear in a mathematical way, which is to say, in the image of human thought. In other words, Nietzsche demonstrates that science is an art that has forgotten that it is an art, and that for it to be true, we first had to create the human being for whom it can be so.

Does this mean that, according to Nietzsche, the philosophers' task is to lie, or, in other words, simply to say whatever they like? This is certainly how some readers have interpreted Nietzsche's sayings that 'there are no truths, there are only interpretations and interpretations of interpretations', and 'if God is dead, then everything is allowed'. And yet we have to be careful. If the modern philosopher thinks of thinking as the establishment in consciousness of relations between clear and distinct ideas, where these find their validity in their relations to facts, then, as soon as these consciousnesses are unchained from facts, they no longer seem to be able to relate to any reality. Thus it seems that they could just say whatever they liked. But Nietzsche argues that thought is not an abstract, 'logical' process taking place in an abstract consciousness and that thought is not a theoretical and indifferent gazing at the world.

Once we realize that God is dead, it becomes impossible to take such an abstract stance with respect to the world. The opposition of truth and lie, understood from such abstraction as acts of consciousness, turns into the concrete opposition of two types of human being: the 'man of reason' and the 'man of intuition'. The latter is the one who has freed his intellect from its enslavement to facts. Looked at from the vantage point of culture, our modern age is the age of the 'man of reason' establishing his dominance over the 'man of intuition' by way of the dominance of science over art, while during the classical Greek age we can see how the artistic spirit has asserted its dominance over its counterpart.

But is Nietzsche not here himself claiming to state true judgements concerning the historical relation between classical Greece and modern Europe? And, if they were not claiming to be true, would they not lose all value at the same time? No: in the same way as Plato, in the famous allegory of the cave, has defined philosophy as the task of liberating the human being from its imprisonment by its superficial beliefs, Nietzsche sees the task of philosophy here as liberating modern human beings from our enslavement to facts. Science says 'This is a fact' and against a fact you cannot argue; you just have to put up with it. Nietzsche answers to this: 'Thus you are advocates of the devil, namely by making of success, of fact, your idol: while a fact is always stupid and has at all times resembled a calf more than a god' (HL 48). In other words, the task of philosophy is not to bring more heavy facts to bear against weaker facts so as to win an argument.

But, again, we need to be careful here. One could too easily think that this claim would amount to an idealistic or even subjective approach to philosophy, which could not be further from the truth. In fact, the notion of facts is directly congruent with the idea of thought as structured through ideas or beliefs. To think of ideas means to think about ideal facts, that is, about clear and distinct ideas. Consequently, to liberate us from the enslavement to facts means at the same time to liberate us from idealism. In short, idealism is essentially chained to materialism as much as the modern natural sciences are chained to Christian theology.

Such an attempt to liberate us from our enchainment to fact seems to the 'man of reason' utterly absurd. To him it appears as a childish illusion, if not even as a malicious lie. In the world of facts there is no human freedom and, as long as only 'scientific' facts count as true, there cannot in principle be a demonstration of freedom. In other words, there cannot be a good argument for it. It is true, we cannot imagine life to be otherwise, but that might just point to the limits of our imagination, rather than to a limit of our possibilities. Thus the task of the philosopher is, first of all, to demonstrate that things can be otherwise, and Nietzsche does this here in two, associated ways: first of all, by demonstrating that things have been otherwise, which is to say that it is at least possible for things to be otherwise, and, second, by showing that things are not quite as they appear to us; that is to say, by arguing that our understanding of life based on factual truths is but a derivation of a life of artistic truth, insofar as all facts have been established and are thus themselves products of artistic creation. In other words, science is art that has forgotten that it is art. The 'truer' life is then that given in artistic falsification.

Nietzsche's claim is that our existence cannot be understood by means of describing what is the case, but that the meaning of that which is the case can only be established by means of a reflection on how it has become what it is. It is in this sense that one can say that with Nietzsche history has become the sole content of philosophy. That the human being has become what it is, shows us that we have to grasp its essence by means of this becoming. If Nietzsche here, in the essay 'On Truth and Lying in an Extra-Moral Sense', seemed merely to have supplied a 'comparison' between two forms of life, what he is really after is the historical sense of existence. To use the above terms of idealism, materialism, theology and modern science as an example: judged as theoretical beliefs concerning the world, they appear essentially different and in opposition, while seen in their historical truth they all appear as interdependent expressions of a Platonist metaphysics of presence.

To understand history as the reality of the world of becoming means that we cannot see it as a well of ideas, that is, as a sequence of stills from which we could extract various ideas, which could then be judged on their own merit. Instead we need a new philosophical methodology which is essentially historical and deals with the historical world as one that never has come to an end and never will come to an end, and which cannot, hence, be understood as moving towards such an end. This method, in his later writings developed under the title of genealogy, thus deals with the world of experience not as consisting of factual truths, but as a constant stream of interpretations and interpretations of interpretations, that is, as the way that human beings deal with all their necessities without being able to direct themselves towards a final truth. If history has no end and no absolute beginning, then we can see the notion of error, that is, the way that humanity errs through its history, as something that can never be overcome in the name of a truth.

The task of the philosopher, which is to say, of all philo-sophia, i.e. of all love of wisdom, is 'to love and to further life for the sake of understanding, and to love and further our errors, our imagination for the sake of life. To give an aesthetic meaning to existence, *to enhance our taste for life* . . .' (KSA9/504).

ii. THE PHILOSOPHER AS PHILOLOGIST AND PHYSICIAN

The philosopher is not somebody who tells the truth for its own sake, but he is the 'extraordinary furtherer of mankind' (BGE § 212, 143). But, as there is no idea of what the human being is, according to which the human being could direct its life, this furtherer of mankind cannot tell human beings what they have to do. Rather his relation to the human being is likened by Nietzsche to that of a physician with respect to the human body. Such a physician does not say what a healthy body ought to do, but she helps the ill body to recover its health, that is, she helps the body to move from incapacity to a self-determining capacity. Equally, the philosopher helps the human being to move from passivity to activity, from enslavement to freedom, without being able or even willing to tell the human being what to do. The first stage on the path to healing is to make the patient realize that she is ill. Thereafter she has to understand the illness and needs to develop an idea of the healing process. These three steps characterize Nietzsche's idea of philosophical teaching. Such teaching cannot take the form of an idea, as it has to be itself a process. If this process is to be successful, it needs to pick up the patient where she is, namely ill, and leave her somewhere else, namely on the path towards good health. For that to happen, both the teaching and the healing have to change in step. The philosopher is thus the 'physician of culture' (7/545).

The first step towards healing is to become aware of the illness one is suffering from. As with medical illnesses, a healing process begins with such a realization, without which one remains passive towards the development of the illness. As far as we modern Europeans are concerned, we often remain unaware of any illness we might be suffering from. We tend to understand our existence as the outcome of a few millennia of progress, so that we see ourselves as more free, more successful, longer living and more prosperous. We understand the human being to be of the highest worth and are supposedly engaged in the universal emancipation of all human beings. And yet, as far as Nietzsche is concerned, our idea of the human being remains restricted to our bare existence, without regard to anything that we have actually done. In other words, our idea of what it is to be human is merely a universal, abstract idea, which can and does easily turn into its opposite. According to this opposite we are biologically determined beings. Our ideas of psychology, morality and politics are oriented by the principles of the modern natural sciences, which is to say that we think of ourselves as pure mechanisms and thus maybe more complex but principally indistinguishable from animal life.

This state of affairs is mirrored in the relation between the ideology of humanism and our scientific world-picture. According to the former, the human being is of an absolute worth, that is to say, a worth that is independent from anything that I do, independent from any becoming. And yet, according to the latter, the human being is just one object in the world amongst others. This problem is outlined quite clearly by the German scientist Werner Heisenberg. In an essay called 'The Development of Philosophical Ideas Since Descartes in Comparison with the New Situation in Quantum Theory', he writes about the necessary consequences of Descartes' denial that the animal has a soul. A soul, as the principle of self-movement, cannot find a place in a mechanical universe. According to Descartes, therefore, only human beings have a soul, but again, a soul which does not inhabit the world of extended things. As Heisenberg argues, such a thought will only take a couple of hundred years to lead to the human being denying the notion of the soul and the idea of human freedom as such. This has happened in nineteenth-century positivism and in twentieth-century behaviourism and is still dominant today in theories of evolutionary psychology, 'biological determinism', etc.

In the late text *The Antichrist*, Nietzsche puts this point in the following words: 'We have found happiness, we know the road, we have found the exit out of whole millennia of labyrinth. Who *else* has found it? – Modern man perhaps? – "I know not which way to turn; I am everything that knows not which way to turn" – sighs modern man. . . . It was from *this* modernity that we were ill . . . (AC § 1). Insofar as Modernity sees itself as the endpoint of progress, it suffers from an understanding of the human being reduced to its sheer existence. But that is to say that freedom is no longer understood as essential action being directed towards the essence of what it means to be human. Freedom is then reduced to the 'freedom of expression', which is as indifferent as that which one might express, namely one's beliefs.

This illness of no longer relating actively to our own being, of no longer seeing a value in our own becoming, thus of the highest values devaluing themselves, Nietzsche calls European Nihilism.

Nihilism, derived from the Latin *nihil*, meaning 'nothing', is that state in which the human being is no longer capable of believing in those values which nonetheless still characterize its existence. While we have considered this here only in the most abstract outlines, what is important to realize is that this notion of an illness is not restricted to the particular beliefs or ideas we might have or might believe in. The nihilist is not the one who professes to have lost faith in God, the soul or any higher values. The one suffering most from nihilism is the one who does not at all realize this illness, who might stick to some vague belief in a Christian God or changes religious affiliation to some other creed, who sticks up for humanist values, for human freedom, the power of scientific truths or equal opportunities for all. In other words, nihilism should not be confused with an individual, psychological phenomenon.

It is for this reason that the first term that Nietzsche gave to this illness was the 'historical malady'. We suffer from having lost our essential relation to history and we suffer from this even and especially where we immerse ourselves in historical studies. As we no longer see our existence in such historical terms, we have reduced it to the abstract universal idea of 'the human being'. Everyone is such a human being, without this word having much more meaning than 'biped' or 'thinking thing'. Thus being restricted to that which is the case, i.e. to being, we lose all relation to becoming. But if that is the case, then, conversely, we can only understand the truth of our existence in answering how we have become what we are. Such a study of history is what Nietzsche understands by philology. In order to be our physician, the philosopher thus has also to be a philologist.

iii. THE PHILOSOPHER AS LEGISLATOR

The image of the philosopher as a physician reflects the most essential understanding of philosophy since its origin in Plato's dialogues. Here the philosopher is seen as the one who cares for the finitude of the human being by liberating it from its shackles of everyday concerns. The philosopher leaves this everyday life, likened by Plato to living in a cave, and ascends to the light of the ideas, to the realm of truth. But he does not remain here and his task does not consist in merely stating truths. Rather he has to be forced to go back into the cave and serve humankind as that which Plato calls the philosopher-king.

That the philosopher is here not merely concerned with speaking the truth can already be seen in that the political task of the philosopher is, for Plato, necessarily unending. While the animal side of the human being belongs to the household, it becomes properly human in its accession to the *agora* – the market square. Here it is human precisely insofar as it is concerned with the question of what it means to be human, which is to say, it is concerned with its own self-determination. The clearest indication of philosophy as such a care for the finitude of the human being can be seen in Plato's treatment of love in the *Symposium*. *Eros* is here understood as the essentially philosophical attitude to life. Philosophy, derived from the Greek words *philos* and *sophia*, is the love of wisdom. Within this love of wisdom, the philosopher understands himself necessarily as the one who, precisely insofar as he desires truth, does not have it. As knowledge is understood as knowledge of the true, and insofar as the true can only be that which is eternally true, the love of knowledge is a love of immortality, which is, for Plato, equally a love for the divine. But, insofar as the human being is understood as the halfway house between heaven and earth, as body and soul, such directing oneself towards the divine is not like just any relation that one entertains to something that one does not have. Rather, this not-having is the most essential trait of human being. Therefore the philosopher, who guides his compatriots in their aligning themselves towards the divine in the political arena, is the one who cares for the essential mortality of the human being.

Platonic thought has thus done two things: first it has given the human being the ability to direct itself to its own being, which is to say that it has opened up the possibility for freedom as self-determination, and, second, it has elevated the desire for knowledge to the most essential property of human existence. Knowledge is thus not something which one might or might not have, but the desire for knowledge is that which makes the human being human. And this is also to say that knowledge is what makes it possible for there to be a world of appearance. While animal nature is fully given over to the constant stream of becoming, in such a way that the animal cannot even see 'some-thing' – a position that still survives in contemporary behaviourism and other ideas of 'biological determinism' – the human being has experiences insofar as it can direct itself towards the eternal truth.

While Nietzsche appears to be opposed to Plato, this and many other fundamental ideas of philosophy survive in his thought. As Nietzsche says, within the general flux of things, the philosopher serves as a 'shoe-drag' (the original German is *Hemmschuh*: the idea is, in other words, that the philosopher's work is opposing oneself to the tide of time) (7/710). In a similar vein he calls Plato the philosopher with the highest *Will to Power*, in that his philosophy stamps the image of being onto becoming. But, more essentially speaking, Nietzsche's conception of the *Eternal Return of the Same* would remain incomprehensible without understanding this notion of philosophy. When undergoing the sudden illumination of the *Eternal Return of the Same* in the year 1881, he described one of its most essential consequences as 'the infinite importance of our knowledge, our errors, of our habits and ways of life for all that is to come' (9/494). This Platonic notion of 'being what we know' rather than just knowing something while remaining essentially indifferent to such knowledge, opens up the Nietzschean under-standing of our world as interpretation. If freedom is understood as self-determination and if our self-determination is understood on this basis of knowledge, then our essential history is nothing but this history of our self-interpretation, which no longer knows anything true apart from what it is, so that this history becomes the erring of human essence through time.

Yet we can see that this position demands that the philosopher is more than a philologist and a physician. If we see the Platonic determination of human essence as a radical incision in history, so that it could give rise to European history as such, then we can see that Plato has not only cared for the finitude of the human being in the way that a doctor might concern herself with the health of the body. First of all, the Greeks did not suffer the same illness that we suffer. But, more essentially, if we can by right call the last two and a half millennia Platonic, if we can call Christianity 'Platonism for the people', then Plato has determined our self-understanding far beyond that which he envisaged. If, as Nietzsche has shown since the essay 'On Truth and Lying in an Extra-Moral Sense', Platonism still gives the form to our understanding of language, of thought, of action and things, then philosophy shows itself, however one might judge this Platonic age, as the most creative discourse. It does not only see what is, it commands what shall be.

From here follows the most exalted understanding of the task of the philosopher in the theatre of history. Nietzsche likens historical life to a theatre play, and wonders where the philosophers belong. They are not on the stage and thus often think of themselves as merely looking at the spectacle, while the way that Plato has created our modern world makes clear that his thought has been much more creative than we could imagine. In fact, in this image the philosopher has to be thought of as the one who writes the play which is then enacted on the stage of history. Thus he says in *The Gay Science*:

[The philosopher] fancies that he is a *spectator* and a *listener* who has been placed before the great visual and acoustic spectacle that is life; he calls his own nature *contemplative* and overlooks that he himself is really the poet who keeps creating this life. Of course, he is different from the *actor* of this drama, the so-called active type; but he is even less like a mere spectator and festive guest in front of the stage. As a poet, he certainly has *vis contemplativa*, and the ability to look back upon his work, but at the same time also and above all *vis creativa*, which the active human being *lacks*, whatever visual appearances and the faith of the world might say. We who think and feel at the same time are those who really continually *fashion* something that had not been there before: the whole eternally growing world of valuations, colours, accents, perspectives, scales, affirmations, and negations. This poem that we have invented is continually studied by the so-called practical human beings (our actors) who learn their roles and translate everything into flesh and actuality, into the everyday. (GS § 301)

While not immediately striking us as a passage that could relate Nietzsche especially to Plato, this description of the philosopher directly translates Plato's thought of the human being as that which has continually to be created. It is thus helpful to remember, against the usual, quite mistaken interpretation of Plato's stance towards the poets, that he excludes the poets from his ideal city precisely because they are doing the same thing as the philosopher, because, as the proverb says, too many cooks spoil the broth. That is to say, the poets are essentially rivals and hence the proper antagonists of the philosopher (817 b6). And one should likewise bear in mind that the meaning of philosophy, insofar as its overarching telos lies in the creation of the philosopher as legislator, is directed at the political, which itself is irreconcilable with our 'objective' idea of truth. That the atheist, according to the *Laws*, should be punished by death, is precisely because he threatens the life of human society with an absolute 'truth', namely the mere givenness of the world. And, insofar as the human being can be threatened by such absolute truth, we can see that, even for Plato, to be human, it is not enough for the human being just to be there, just to exist; it needs to be free, in the sense of relating to its own essence.

To stay with the image of the theatre, we can see that the philosopher as the scriptwriter of history is not seen or heard directly. If the play is good, the audience believes that the actors speak with their own voices. Equally, the commanding of which Nietzsche speaks is not done with a commanding voice. Nietzsche expresses this fateful idea of philosophical thinking in the *Zarathustra*. In his 'Stillest Hour' some voiceless voice speaks to Zarathustra and asks him: 'Of what consequence are you?'. When Zarathustra answers with insecurity, the voice responds:

'Do you know what it is all men most need? Him who commands great things. To perform great things is difficult: but more difficult is to command great things.

This is the most unpardonable thing about you: You have the power and you will not rule.' (Z 168)

Having thus referred himself back to the Platonic notion of the philosopher-king, the voice clarifies our misunderstanding concerning the role of such a philosopher-king as a self-centred tyrant:

. . . And I answered: 'I lack the lion's voice for command'.

Then again something said to me as in a whisper: 'It is the stillest words which bring the storm. Thoughts that come on doves' feet guide the world'. (Z 168)

iv. FREEDOM AND FATUM: NIETZSCHE'S BODY

Therefore, my reader, I am myself the matter of my book: there is no reason for you to invest your spare time in such a frivolous and vain subject. Goodbye, then; from Montaigne . . .

Montaigne

We have seen the problem of philosophical thinking after the death of God. This was shown most clearly in that we are still Platonic enough to base our thought on the Platonic idea of the human being as the halfway house between heaven and earth; and yet, we no longer believe in this heaven and hence, mostly without knowing, we no longer believe in ourselves. We certainly exist, but consider ourselves to belong to that mechanical system of determinate motion which we call nature. The whole of modern philosophical thought since Descartes is afflicted with this problem, whether it appears as a mind–body problem or, with Immanuel Kant, as the incompatibility between theoretical and practical knowledge.

But, again, if human knowledge cannot exceed this world of constant change, how can one make any philosophical claims? How could one even understand the human being to be transcendent, that is, to step over the boundaries of that which is immediately given, in order then to speak from such a position? How can the philosopher be possible at all once we no longer believe in the transcendence of freedom?

Often we ask another, though similar, question, when we calculate, against Nietzsche, that it is incoherent to say that 'there is no truth', insofar as we happily exclaim that if this sentence is to be true, then it contradicts the claim it makes, while if it is not supposed to be true, then it is, obviously, wrong. While we intuitively know that this argument concerning logical contradiction is quite meaningless, we are more accustomed to a similar existential contradiction, as, for example, when somebody says 'I am a biological determinist'. Such a sentence presumes that I can transcend immediate reality in order to form a theory, while the content of the theory denies precisely this ability. But does not Nietzsche's text perform a similar contradiction? Many readers are confused as to whether Nietzsche might himself be a determinist, while others take him to be an individualist, exalting the creative freedom of the human being. It is quite strange: following the death of God, everything seems to be possible, while it was precisely the idea of a supersensible existence that made freedom possible in the first place. Consequently one can now think anything while nothing has any meaning. The 'biological determinist' thus says: 'I think that in truth there is no truth beyond simple factual states'. But can Nietzsche say more than this?

Let us look again at the problem as it is given in Descartes' separation of a thinking thing and an extended thing, i.e. of mind and body. Here the human essence as given between heaven and earth, between freedom and necessity has become reified, which is to say that both mind and body are called things. The soul harbours the notion of human freedom, but this has here become passive: it merely represents the truth by means of positive, affirmative judgements. The 'biological determinist' is the expression of such a Cartesian truth, of a Platonism devoid of its activity. Here the mind looks at a body that is his and realizes that there is no truth in it. The freedom of this mind consists in the mere ability of stating that it is in chains. Equally, when we think about the human spirit by way of metaphors like hardware and software, we are Cartesians, who think of both body and mind as things. The contemporary task of philosophy for Nietzsche is thus to overcome idealism as much as materialism, the notion of a freedom of choice as much as the idea of determinism.

But, considering what we said about the unavailability of a truth independent of the world, considering that we said we could hardly speak and communicate unless words had a true meaning, how should such philosophizing be possible? Often we see the ideal of the teacher as a divine person, as someone who knows it all and benevolently gives away her knowledge. Thus, for example, it has been argued that Nietzsche did not believe in the *Eternal Return of the Same*, because Zarathustra did not teach this idea following the section 'On the Face and Riddle' in the *Zarathustra*. But this is again to presuppose without questioning that teaching can only take the form of affirming abstract representations. These are thought to be 'ideal-things' representing 'real-things', where the first belong to the mind, the second to the world of bodies. And these representations can be objective, precisely insofar as mind and body are conceived as two independent substances.

From the insight that God is dead it thus follows for Nietzsche that we have to give up both on the ideal of a true world and the representation of a world of brute facts. We have already encountered the clearest statement to this effect: 'We have abolished the true world: which world is left? The apparent world, perhaps? . . . But no, with the true world we have also abolished the apparent world' (6/81). As a consequence we can no longer think of thinking either as an ideal process within consciousness, or as the combination in the mind of universal terms and particulars that are given in experience and grasped by these terms. After the death of God and the end of metaphysical values, this kind of thinking is no longer available to us. Neither objective nor subjective, neither idealist nor materialist, how should thinking be thought of at all?

Nietzsche's answer to this question centres around the human body. This body is not a particular instance of a universal idea, rather it is the individual, living body as the locus of thought. To look at the world, so to speak, from within, makes us turn to the body no longer as a mechanical entity but as the living medium of existence itself. If all there is, is history itself, then the body becomes the central thought of philosophy:

> *Following the Guide of the Living Body.* – Taken that 'the soul' was an attractive and enigmatic thought, which, with reason, philosophers have only reluctantly given up – maybe that which they will learn to trade for it is even more attractive, even more enigmatic. The human body, in which the whole of the farthest and nearest past of all organic becoming reawakens and becomes body, through which and beyond which an enormous but inaudible stream seems to flow: the living body is a more stupendous thought than the old 'soul'. (11/565)

The living body is essentially different from the mechanical body of biology or physics. This difference is a bit clearer in the German distinction between *Körper* (body) and *Leib* (living body), and it is here clarified by its historical dimension. While a physical body is given in the present, as an object of investigation and hence purely factual, the living body is essentially historical. In it 'the whole of the farthest and nearest past of all organic becoming reawakens and becomes body' and it is thus with respect to the body that we can gain a distance from the world of immediate things. In other words, while the Christian tradition of thought has dealt with the notion of freedom as a metaphysical idea, available only to the immaterial soul, for Nietzsche freedom becomes possible only on account of the body.

Nietzsche has discovered that mind and body are one. Consequently, 'most of our thinking happens totally undetected by consciousness', or 'consciousness is but the tip of the iceberg of what we call thinking'. If one thus credits Nietzsche with the discovery of the unconscious, one has to bear in mind that this unconscious is precisely modelled not on the notion of consciousness, but on the living body as a locus of drives and instincts. Philosophy first of all gains weight through this discovery; it becomes much more important than one has thought before, when still mistaking it for free juggling with abstract ideas. This is one of the most important neglects of the philosophical tradition: that it has confined all thinking and feeling to the opposition of rationality and irrationality, while neither helps much in explaining the world of our deeds and 'things'.

Against the tradition Nietzsche attempts to understand thought as a bodily process, as something which depends on an atmosphere in which it can develop and on account of which it can no longer be understood as self-founding. Consequently Nietzsche understands thought as already grounded in the dark, which is to say in non- or pre-reflexive processes. For that reason he often speaks of a physiology of thought and understands the philosopher as the one 'who thinks and feels at the same time'.

But if the body is not a simple object taken into consideration by a consciousness – that is, if it cannot be understood as a causal nexus of facts – then it opens onto the thought of a world of becoming, of constant change. Such change understood in a more concrete sense is the world of history. But insofar as it is thus impossible to look at the world of history from the outside, and insofar as thought cannot ever become fully transparent to itself, then the history of the body necessarily opens up the thought of history as fate. Nietzsche first discovered this idea of linking the understanding of the body with a notion of fate as an adolescent when reading Ralph Waldo Emerson's works, which led him to write two essays on 'Fatum and History' and 'Free Will and Fatum' (KSA J 2/54–63). While these essays adumbrate these notions quite hazily, in that they still rely on the notions of soul and spirit, and on the opposition of fate and freedom, of conscious action and unconscious action, they already posit the necessary relation of free will to fate, without which freedom would become groundless and abstract. These essays also already contrast the viewpoint of fatalism as strength of character to the weakness characterizing the Christian world view.

While there is not much discussion of the body in these essays, they nonetheless reflect on habits and historical tradition as the underlying reality of thought. In Emerson's essays, with which Nietzsche said that he had never felt 'so at home and in my home' (9/588), he found not only his ideal of a philosopher, of he 'who moves according to self-created laws, makes up his own tables of the values of men and things and who overthrows those which existed and who *represents the law in his own person*' (9/671), but also the following remark on the relation between individual and history:

Man is explicable by nothing less than all his history. . . . A man is the whole encyclopaedia of facts. . . . If the whole of history is in one man, it is all to be explained from individual experience. There is a relation between the hours of our life and the centuries of time. . . . the hours should be instructed by the ages, and the ages explained by the hours. (History 3f)

Although Emerson speaks here of the relation between the universal mind in which the individual partakes and nature, the examples he provides liken, for example, the 'furrow of the brow' to 'strata of rock'; they speak of Händel's ears or the 'constructive fingers' of Watt, thereby leading Nietzsche more and more towards the historical reality of the body as an individuated historical reality.

While the idea of an objective truth has led philosophy to denounce any statement whose truth depends on the individual who utters it as 'psychologism' – that is, as a statement devoid of any truth insofar as it merely expresses the state of a single subject and remains relative to this subject – with Nietzsche philosophy becomes a strange kind of biography or somatography; that is, a written account of one's life insofar as it is written within one's body. As it is thus not the individual psyche that here writes about its life, the truth here discovered is not a purely subjective truth, but the truth of *our* world. As we have said above, philosophy, since its inception, has understood itself as the war against common sense, against beliefs, and it was in this context that the argument of psychologism made sense. But are we really looking at Nietzsche's life, which, as has been rightly said, was neither particularly pleasant nor beautiful? Obviously not. Nietzsche's thought cannot be seen as an expression of his body in such a sense. The life that he speaks of is given to itself in intuition. When Nietzsche says that the philosopher is always turned to two sides, to the world on the one hand and to himself on the other (7/712), then we can see now that this is not simply the ambivalence of a conscious attitude, but necessary on account of the reason of philosophical thinking. This reason is not abstractly logical but derives from the body itself, from that which within it is its destiny. In other words, to say that the product of the philosopher is his life (7/712) is not to say that he creates like a god. There is here no *creatio ex nihilo*, but an attentiveness to that which is necessary. The following two quotations, from *The Gay Science* and the *Zarathustra*, clarify these points sufficiently:

We philosophers are not free to divide body from soul as the people do; we are even less free to divide soul from spirit. We are not thinking frogs, nor objectifying and registering mechanisms with their innards removed: constantly, we have to give birth to our thoughts out of our pain and, like mothers, endow them with all we have of blood, heart, fire, pleasure, passion, agony, conscience, fate, and catastrophe. (GS 347f)

And:

'I am body and soul' – so speaks the child. And why should one not speak like children?

But the awakened, the enlightened man says: I am body entirely, and nothing beside; and soul is only a word for something in the body.

The body is a great reason, a multiplicity with one sense, a war and a peace, a herd and a herdsman. Your small reason, my brother, which you call 'spirit', is also an instrument of your body, a little instrument and toy of your great reason. (Z 61f)

The 'strife' between these two forms of reason is what we experience in that which, since Descartes, we call the 'mind–body problem'. The age in which philosophers oppose these to one another is a nihilistic age. Here the 'small reason' attempts to dominate the 'great reason'; philosophers appear as 'despisers of the body', while it is only the 'great reason' that is able to understand Nietzsche's thinking. The 'small reason', which we call the abstract, concentrated mind, must of necessity remain indifferent, disdainful with respect to any thought. When Nietzsche says that knowledge is a strife within the thinker, then it is not only the strife between different truths, but also this strife between these two reasons. And that it is a strife rather than just a judgement, is because the 'great reason', the body, has to deny the idea of consciousness as the indifferent arbitrator over questions of truth.

Again we can see that Nietzsche's turn against traditional philosophy is more sophisticated than it at first appears. Where philosophy based itself on the notion of reason, Nietzsche does not demand 'unreason', but an understanding of the 'great reason'. When philosophy since Socrates argues that all true knowledge has to begin with knowledge of the self, Nietzsche does not simply turn this around, but makes clear to us that we have not yet even started to understand this self. Let us look at this more carefully. Socrates founded philosophical thinking on self-knowledge:

> I investigate not these things [general questions about the nature of the universe, etc.], but myself, to know whether I am a monster more complicated and more furious than Typhoon or a gentler and simpler creature, to whom a divine and quiet lot is given by nature. (Phaedrus 230a)

In the time since those days we can see the rise of the sciences as the systematic grounding of our knowledge of nature on the basis of the subjectivity of the subject. Consequently, Immanuel Kant, one of the founders of the modern sciences, has shown that the sciences can be absolutely objective once we realize that we 'do not take the law from nature but prescribe it to nature' (*Prolegomena* § 36, p. 79). It thus appears that the whole of European thought is the attempt at a reasonable foundation of the self, until, again in the humanism of Immanuel Kant, the whole world appears to turn around the human being.

It is, then, quite surprising to read the *Genealogy of Morality*, which Nietzsche begins with the following reflection:

> We are unknown to ourselves, we knowers, we ourselves, to ourselves, and there is a good reason for this. We have not looked for

ourselves, – so how are we ever supposed to *find* ourselves? . . .
We remain strange to ourselves out of necessity, we do not
understand ourselves, we *must* confusedly mistake who we are
. . . (GM 3)

How is it possible to say that 'we have not looked for ourselves',
considering that all philosophy is an attempt at understanding the
world based on knowledge of the self? We have seen it already,
because we have confused our self with the abstract notion of an
indifferent 'consciousness'. But everyone is such a 'self', such an 'I',
and all we understand here is 'the I in general', the subject as the
pure form of subjectivity as such and in general. The mistake was,
then, to identify the 'I' with an abstract notion of consciousness,
which is not at all necessary for life. Indeed, 'the whole of life would
be possible without, as it were, seeing itself in a mirror' (GS § 354).
It is on account of such a mistake that we fail to understand our
existence in its concrete form. We think of the 'human being', of
reason or understanding, in universal, abstract terms and therefore
miss the concretion of our existence and the historical nature of
thinking itself. In order to understand ourselves, we would have to
find the key opening the prison of consciousness. Indeed, what do
we know about ourselves?

Does nature not remain silent about almost everything, even
about our bodies, banishing and enclosing us within a proud,
illusory consciousness, far away from the twists and turns of the
bowels, the rapid flow of the blood stream and the complicated
tremblings of the nerve-fibres? Nature has thrown away the key,
and woe betide fateful curiosity should it ever succeed in peering
through a crack in the chamber of consciousness, out and down
into the depths, and thus gain an intimation of the fact that
humanity, in the indifference of its ignorance, rests on the pitiless,
the greedy, the insatiable, the murderous. (TL 142)

One great exception to this imprisonment in consciousness
Nietzsche finds in the thought of Gottfried Wilhelm Leibniz. While
we might have expected Nietzsche's thought to be the antithesis of
all rationalism, it is precisely the three great rationalists, namely
Leibniz, Spinoza and Hegel, who have the most marked influence on
Nietzsche's thought. One might superficially object that Leibnizian

thought presupposes the idea of a pre-established harmony of all beings as created by God, that Spinoza's philosophy depends on the geometrical understanding of reason, that Hegel's system understands itself as a panlogism, and that consequently all these are quite incompatible with Nietzsche's text. And yet, philosophy does not decide its position on the level of ideas. Nietzsche is certainly not a rationalist, neither does he assemble a theory out of ideas which he indiscriminately finds here, there or anywhere. We can already draw the consequence from the above that if thought does not look down onto the earth, if it is located within the historically constituted living body, then the question is not so much how one can hit on any truth, but rather how one should be able to get anything completely wrong. Indeed, with respect to the body nothing is wrong, while the heart is certainly more valuable than the appendix.

In other words, every great philosophy expresses its truth, or, here as elsewhere, 'the errors of great men are worthy of reverence, because they are more productive than the truths of the small men' [KSA J 3/353]. And yet, in opposition to Descartes, who only seems to figure as the greatest error, and to Kant, whom Nietzsche sees as giving the clearest expression to this error, with Leibniz, Spinoza and Hegel Nietzsche finds a lineage of thought giving rise to himself. In Leibniz he finds the exposition of the freedom of the will as fatalism, in Spinoza the understanding of knowledge as the highest affect and in Hegel the discovery of history as the reality of all becoming. And, indeed, the influence of Leibniz pervades Nietzsche's whole thought, from the notion of freedom, of the will and of life, right through to the notion of time as arising from the finite will opening up to the infinity of its willing.

We were asking why Nietzsche claims that the philosophers have never looked for themselves, and found an answer in that they were mostly thinking about reason as such, about consciousness as such, while Frank, Mary or Joseph – that is, individuals who cannot be reduced to being an instance of a universal – do not seem to exist for philosophy. In Descartes we find an *ego cogito* as *res cogitans*, which is to say, an 'I think' as a 'thinking thing', but there is nothing that we can say about this and there is nothing which could individuate this thinking thing. In Kant we find the 'I' as that which accompanies every representation, but this appears as a mute and undifferentiated being accompanying us, a form of subjectivity as such and in general, without any individuality. Looking at the 'I' in this way, how should we ever come to know ourselves? Leibniz, on the other hand, argues for the existence of individual substances, which is to say, for the irreducible existence of, for example, Frank, Mary and Joseph. Let us attempt to understand the main points of Leibniz's system insofar as they are significant for Nietzsche's thought.

Rationalism in the emphatic sense of the word argues that the reason for which we know what the world is, is the same as the reason for which the world is what it is; in short, it identifies knowing and being. Therefore rationalism is necessarily a monism, arguing that there is only one substance. Thus Leibniz does not confront the active mind with a passive nature. If there is only one kind of substance, there must be a good reason for choosing one or the other. It seems, as Leibniz says, that it is difficult to establish such a reason, so that both the thought that there is finally only passive matter – leading to various forms of 'materialism' – and the thought that, finally, every phenomenon can be led back to manifestations of an active mind – giving rise to various forms of 'idealism' – appear to be consistent. But, if one really could choose between them, then idealism would present itself as the more persuasive, as it would give rise to the understanding of the world on account of freedom and meaning, as opposed to the materialist understanding of a determined world, which finally remains without any meaning.

But we do not have to remain on this abstract level of arbitration. Leibniz, one of the last universal geniuses, who worked in all the various fields of philosophical thought, in metaphysics as much as in mathematics, in theology as much as in natural philosophy, is, together with Isaac Newton and Immanuel Kant, one of the fathers of the modern natural sciences. The important shift in these sciences is that nature is no longer seen as an order of 'objects' or things, but understood in terms of the notion of force. Natural reality is not made up of extended objects, but of forces, which are defined not by extension, but by their mathematical values. The main difference between a force and, say, the idea of an atom, is that a force cannot be thought of in isolation from other forces. In other words, a force cannot be represented passively, as 'just' being there, before it then would 'do' anything. The idea of a force is that of an essentially active entity, which is equal to its expression, or, which is nothing besides its expression. Furthermore, such expression is possible only in being related to another force. This is why Newton discovered that each force is countered by another force of equal value and that the sum total of all forces in the universe always remains equal to itself. It is this fundamental shift in the understanding of nature that characterizes modern physics and that, consequently, will serve Nietzsche as a foundation for the elaboration of the doctrine of the *Eternal Return of the Same*.

With this notion of force nature has become something essentially active. If, for example, we think of a big boulder in a Cartesian world, this boulder is understood as something essentially passive. It just lies around somewhere. Indeed, if we were to kick it, it should fly away. With the discovery of force, on the other hand, this boulder is now understood through the notion of action. The idea of inertia, of the resistance of the boulder to our kick, makes us understand passivity as 'relative' activity, or, say, as re-action. As Leibniz says, 'something passive could not exist even for a second'. While we are obviously not too surprised about this insight, as it has shaped the last few centuries of the modern sciences, the further consequences that Leibniz draws from here are perhaps more astounding.

The scientist might think that the world can be understood as a nexus of forces moved through time by that which we call natural causation. There is a certain state of affairs and by means of causal connection this gives rise to another state of affairs. This is even our idea of determinism, namely that the meaning of any given state of affairs is to be found in its cause – which is to say, in its past. And yet, such interpretation contravenes the insight that we have just described. A force is something essentially active, while thinking of it as an effect of a prior force, which in turn is seen as an effect of a prior cause, means that one has stealthily returned the interpretation of forces to the notion of passivity. While this ruse might allow us to represent these states of affairs in their 'factual truth', the reality of force has again escaped us. This is where Leibniz locates the difference between the scientific and the philosophical understanding of the world. The scientist might restrict himself to such understanding. While it is essentially mistaken, it still affords us useful insights into nature. The philosopher, on the other hand, needs to go further. If the essence of force is activity, while a given force as represented in its effects on other forces in the world of nature again appears passive, then the essence of force must be something different from its expression within space and time.

This essence Leibniz calls the *monad*, which is to say, in Greek, the one and indivisible entity. For our purposes we might here call it the will or the soul. The monad is, then, the metaphysical truth of the physical force. Insofar as there are innumerable forces making up physical reality, there are equally innumerable monads and, as these are essentially active, they cannot be seen as the effects of other forces. In other words, the monad is not in time and space, but time and space are representations within each monad. Nothing happens to a monad, but everything that has happened, is happening or will happen to it, is part of its full conception. Or, rather, the only events that happen to a monad happen to it through God – that is, the creation of the monad and its destruction – but these are not events within its existence. Each monad consists, then, of the representation of its whole world from its proper perspective within itself. The monad can thus be called an individual substance.

Every individuated, organic existence, like 'Karl', for example, can be understood as a relation between a given number of monads. There are the forces governing digestion, movement of the limbs, breathing, conscious representation, etc. Each of these points towards a monad as their metaphysical reality. But have we not just said that monads are not in time and space, that they do not seem to be able to make up an organism? Have we not said that monads do not relate to each other, that there is no causal power of one over the other? Leibniz's answer is that they do not need to. Insofar as God has created all monads, the relation between these is not a question of a physical relation but one of representational harmony. Each monad *is* the representation of the world from its specific perspective in a more or less active manner, whereby we can see that 'the world' is not something existing in a real sense outside of them. Rather, the world 'as such' exists only in the mind of God as the totality of all the different perspectives of all monads. This is what Leibniz calls 'pre-established harmony'.

What does this mean for 'Karl'? First of all, that he need not see his active mind in opposition to a passive, material body. All is, so to speak, will or mind, with the differences between monads given in their degree of activity. The conscious mind, that which we tend to call the soul, is the most active of all these monads. It has a broader perspective; it represents more of its being. A force of the digestive system, on the other hand, is much less aware of itself. And yet, every monad is nothing but such representation, whatever degree of awareness it might have of this. From here Nietzsche draws his understanding of the prevalence of the 'great reason': it is '*Leibniz*' incomparable insight . . . that consciousness is merely an *accidens* of experience and *not* its necessary and essential attribute; that . . . what we call consciousness constitutes only one state of our spiritual and psychic world . . . and *not by any means the whole of it*' (GS 305). This insight gives rise to the concrete notion of the body.

Although Leibniz speaks here of monads, not of the body, these monads are, first of all, explanations of the reality of such body. And for the thinker to know herself, she no longer needs to leave the reality of this world to move towards universal truths, but has to return to her living body as the real existence of the world itself. When Nietzsche speaks of drives and instincts as historical sedimentations, when he says that 'you are *Will to Power* and nothing besides, and this world is *Will to Power* and nothing besides', this becomes intelligible only on account of this understanding of the will as the underlying reality of all existence.

Having made this detour through Leibniz, we can now return to our main thread illuminating the relation between freedom, fate and the body. The 'scientist', as Leibniz said, understands the world as essentially a deterministic play of forces in which there is no intrinsic meaning and to which thought and freedom remain alien. In this representation the essentially active reality of force is perverted into something passive. In such a world I understand myself as something passive. The world often appears only as the sum total of all the things that hinder my own expression. This world is full of suffering; events happen to me, restricting my freedom. The move of the intellect from this phenomenal reality to that which Leibniz calls the intelligible reality of the monads changes everything. Here the monad radically escapes determination. Whatever happens is an actualization of my own existence. My happiness is no longer contingent on an affirmation of a world outside of my powers, nor on abstract notions of a freedom of choice. Insofar as everything that has happened, is happening and will happen belongs to my very being, the choice that makes my freedom a reality is that for or against myself. Retrospectively one might here already hear Nietzsche's dictum concerning the reality of freedom in the choice to 'become the one who you are'. Here a notion of freedom as authenticity, as choosing oneself, is contrasted to our abstract notion of a freedom of choice. In short, freedom appears here in the form of *amor fati*, as the love of fate, and fatalism thus appears as the opposite of determinism.

As this all sounds rather abstract, let us briefly consider two examples, one given by Leibniz himself in the *Discourse on Metaphysics* and the other one by the French author Denis Diderot in his novel *Jacques the Fatalist*. In the former, Leibniz reflects on the moral significance of Judas' betrayal of Jesus Christ. Certainly, it first appears to Judas, on account of deliberation, that the act he should commit is to betray the confidence that Jesus has invested in him. He does so, with the consequence of the arrest and consequent crucifixion of Christ. It is the actual deed that changes his understanding of it. What appeared justified in deliberation now seems unjustified in reality. Experiencing this incompatibility of the act thought of and the act committed, Judas is filled with remorse and guilt. And yet, consequently, his apprehension changes.

Was his indeed an evil deed? It certainly appears as such having even become the paradigmatic act of betrayal. And yet, it appears also as an act conceived of by someone other than himself. Was not 'his' betrayal a necessary part of the revelation of God? If he had not betrayed Jesus Christ, the latter could never have become Jesus Christ, which is to say the one who by dying on the cross signified the becoming flesh of God. Suddenly what first seemed to be a good course of action, having turned into an evil reality, again appears as good. But that only signifies that the deliberation preceding the act might have been mistaken. On account of a wrong deliberation, the act turned out well. And yet, Judas realizes as well that his act did not at all depend on the act of deliberation. God would not have left the fate of the world to such a coincidence. Indeed, what Judas experiences here is what the French philosopher Jean-Paul Sartre will later refer to with the expression 'deliberation is bad faith', meaning that to base a justification of an act on the idea of deliberation – i.e. 'this, my deed was justified for this and that good logical reason, and because I thought about this, I did it' – is to cover over a real motivation by an ideal, imagined reason, which absolves me from responsibility. I am asked: 'Why did you do this?' and answer that 'it is not me who is responsible, as there were good reasons to act as I did'. Judas realizes that he did not make up his deed but that it was already ordained; that, as with the tragic deeds of classical Greek tragedy, all that happened was that he followed his fate, a fate that brought him to ruin. Quite contradictorily his defence against the accusation of having committed evil could be based on the claims that: a) no evil act has been committed as the act of betrayal has led to the greater good of the Revelation; and b) he could not have done otherwise and cannot thus be called guilty.

The most significant insight follows from this contradiction: logically speaking he is now absolved from responsibility, and yet this leaves him with nothing, insofar as his whole life now appears empty. He could not have done otherwise; he could neither have become the most loyal follower of Christ, nor can he boast about his cunning in devising the act of betrayal. All that remains is that he is the one who betrayed Jesus Christ. And the only choice he has left is either to affirm or to deny this, his very being. To 'become the one who he is' thus means to take this being onto himself, that is, to come to love his fate. Here in Leibniz's account of Judas we can find the beginning of a long tradition in philosophical thinking, developed in Hegel's, then in Nietzsche's and more recently in Heidegger's and Sartre's philosophies, in each case sharply contrasting the notion of freedom as authenticity to the abstract notion of a freedom of choice.

It is not difficult to see here the tragic world view that Nietzsche had investigated in many essays written during the 1870s. Nor is it difficult to see the relation between Leibniz's example of Judas and the famous tragedy of Oedipus, who unwittingly kills his father and marries his mother, having to take over the responsibility for these actions even though he did not know what he was doing. The story of Oedipus is paradigmatic insofar as it dwells on the fact that first his parents and then he himself try to escape this fate, while this escape shows itself after the fact as essential to this fate as such. In other words, whatever one does, one cannot escape one's fate; the world cannot be otherwise, and all that is left is to affirm or to denounce this life.

Might one not object that such an idea of fatalism only gives a pinkish tint to a bad realization, namely that one has not got any choice about one's actions? What distinguishes such an idea of fatalism from the more materialistic idea of determinism? Sure, one might say that the determinist loses himself in the world, that he cannot find any significance in his existence, as any meaning has always already sunk into the past, while the fatalist finds himself in the world of his deeds. But the real difference is again not one of deliberation, of thinking about myself in the world, but of action. We have seen above that Leibniz understands the world in terms of the notion of activity. Something has the more reality the more active it is and, conversely, something passive could not exist for even a second. This notion of activity has led us away from the prevalence of the 'small reason', the abstract concentrated mind, as the determining point of our existence. To measure the success of any idea of freedom, we thus have to see how it changes the activity of the actor. An experience of this kind is described in Denis Diderot's *Jacques the Fatalist*. This novel mainly follows the events in the lives of two characters, the valet Jacques and his master. They travel through France, discussing philosophical matters, whereby the former attempts to convince his master that everything that happens and any deed one may do has already been written down in 'the book' which lies in heaven.

At one moment of the novel, Jacques and his master arrive at a little inn and sit down to eat. Suddenly marauding soldiers, armed and dangerous, enter the inn and demand that all food and wine is served to them only. Everyone keeps a low profile, looking elsewhere, while the proprietor does as commanded. Then Jacques gets out of his seat, attacking the soldiers. As they are taken completely by surprise, he somehow manages to lock them into an adjacent room before they realize what has happened to them. Returning to his seat, his master, shivering and without any blood left in his face, asks him how he could possibly have endangered his own life and happiness in this way, and Jacques, as one might have expected, answers him that he did not have any choice, that it said in the book that this was what he would do and that he thus did it.

In this novel, as in Nietzsche's early 'Fatum and History', the fatalist is portrayed as the most active human being, and, that is to say, as the most free. While the master, the proponent of an idea of freedom of choice, appears throughout as a weak character, who never acts as he is always afraid of doing something wrong, Jacques simply acts. Here the distinction between the determinist and the fatalist appears most clearly. If Jacques were a determinist, he would not act at all. First, because nothing could be called an action, being devoid of meaning, and, second, because the determinist would constantly have to say 'I did not act: it was my selfish genes', for example. The fatalist, by contrast, finds himself in his actions, the meaning of which is his own existence.

Returning to Leibniz, we can find in his thought most of the features of Nietzsche's philosophy of life. There are the individual substances experiencing their existence in the highest sense of freedom as fate. There is the move towards understanding the whole of existence from this idea of freedom in order to escape the coarse dualism between active and passive substances, and there is, therefore, the attempt to grasp the world in its truth as free from mechanical causation while still from the position of force as it characterizes the rise of the age of classical science. It is for this reason that Leibniz's thought is compatible with even twentieth-century physics, while escaping its deterministic atmosphere.

And yet the Leibnizian monad is an idea of an individual substance conceived as soul or as mind. In other words, Leibniz is an idealist, which is to say that he thinks of truth as belonging to the soul alone. In the end, as he argues, truth can only be truth insofar as it escapes the accidental nature of experience. Moving from science to philosophy thus means to realize that in truth, any possible accidence inheres in the subject in question, which is to say that all truth is necessarily tautological. To say this more clearly, fatalism is here the idea of a pure being oneself. The ideal for such an abstract, self-concentrated mind is pure self-subsistence, actualizing itself through itself. We have seen this already in that the world and the expanse of space and time are mere representations internal to the monad. Its only pathos is to have been created by God and to know that it will in turn be destroyed by God.

The ideal of the monad consists thus in pure self-affection, finding the world wholly within itself. Should this world, turning against this understanding, ever impinge on it, the monad will instinctively turn to passivity, or, insofar as this is not possible for something essentially active, to reaction. Life understanding itself in this way will, as in Darwin, come to understand its primal force as a will to self-preservation, and thus as a passive will defending itself against the world. Yet this, as Nietzsche will argue, is absurd. Replacing Leibniz's God with the idea of an effective history, and thus the soul with the body – replacing, thus, the notion of pre-established harmony with the frightful abyss between truth and art or, again in other words, replacing divine with human creation – changes the notion of the will completely. No longer understood as the metaphysical reality of force, the will as body remains essentially active. It is not self-will but realizes itself in pure affection, which is to say, as relation to the world. To speak of a pure affectivity here means that the body does not allow for the opposition of inside and outside, of inner truth and outward expression.

Indeed, such opposition of inside and outside Nietzsche continuously denounces as a consequence of Roman culture – that is to say, of decadence. All that the body does is act and it *is* these actions and nothing besides. Put more simply, while an abstract mind can be understood as being the more free the more it is independent from the world, the body is the more free the more it can relate itself to the world. We will see this in much more detail when turning to the notion of the *Will to Power*. Here it suffices to understand the relation between the body and the philosophizing of Nietzsche as based on the notion of fate, i.e. as not transcending the plane of history, as an actualization of freedom in the attempt to become the one who one is.

We have seen that the notion of fate allows for an affirmation of life. Precisely because one does not brood about how things might have turned out otherwise, because one does not flee oneself but finds oneself, can the experience of freedom that we do have find expression in the way that we live in the world. Even little examples might illuminate the point. If one considers moving to another country on account of a highly idealized image that one has of this country, the likelihood is that one will come to regret it. Nothing can ever live up to such expectations and finally one starts to resent all the various shortcomings. If, on the other hand, one ends up in the very same place, never having planned or contemplated such a move beforehand, putting it down to fate, to circumstances which never made clear where they might lead, the likelihood is that one is more able to affirm this life. In Leibniz this affirmation takes the form of the realization that this world is the best of all possible worlds. This judgement does not derive from a comparison of many possible worlds, but mainly from the understanding of divine creation. Leibniz's affirmation that this is the best of all possible worlds hence remains purely formal. Nietzsche derides this solution to the problem of an affirmation of life on account of its abstraction. Reading Dühring's *The Value of Life* from 1865, he notes: 'Whether this be the best of all worlds is an absurd question: we have no idea of variant possibilities' (8/134).

The tragic affirmation of life, on the other hand, can justify 'the existence of even the "worst of all worlds" ' (BT § 25, p. 115), and it can do so precisely because it does not suffer from the separation of mind and body. Insofar as Greek tragedy sees the notion of fate with respect to the body, its affirmation does not restrict itself to the pure form of an ideal judgement, but is itself a striving, a practical valuation which is, in its striving, identical with that which it judges. As Spengler shows quite convincingly in his *The Decline of the West*, the classical, Greek understanding of fatalism rests, not on the philosophical distinction between instances and universals, with its idealistic tendencies, but on the 'empirical I', that is, on the body or, in Greek, the *soma*. Thus 'Oedipus complains that Kreon has violated his *living body* and that the oracle concerns his *living body*' (*Decline* 169). It is this centrality of the body with respect to the tragic affirmation of life that places Nietzsche in opposition to idealism as much as materialism, to traditional philosophy as much as the modern natural sciences.

From the elucidation of this relation between freedom, *amor fati* and the body, we are now in a position to understand much more clearly the following two points. These concern Nietzsche's so-called 'irrationalism' and his sometimes irritating megalomania. That there is something wrong about these accusations is already clear in that Nietzsche often seems to be embodying the opposite, namely a relentless reasoning and a radical modesty. But again, these appear as contradictions only from the perspective of the understanding. Let us clarify this point. We read in his auto-biography *Ecce Homo*, in the fourth chapter, entitled 'Why I am a Destiny':

> I know my fate. One day the memory of something uncanny will be attached to my name, – to a crisis as there never has been on earth, to the deepest collision of conscience, to a decision evoked against everything that has hitherto been believed, demanded and held sacred. I am not a human being, I am dynamite. (6/365)

Such a sentence must, from the perspective of the understanding, remain quite meaningless. Insofar as the understanding functions analytically, its ideal is mechanism. This is to say that the understanding has understood something as soon as it has identified its cause. Indeed, that we can think of truth as the adequation between a sentence and a state of fact, is possible precisely insofar as we here understand the linguistic relation between subject and predicate in analogy to the 'physical' relation between cause and effect. This is also the reason why the understanding will never be able to understand an act of freedom, insofar as an act related to its cause is also understood as a dependent act. This is why, traditionally, the question of freedom has been understood as a metaphysical or theological question, and later, especially in the critical philosophy of Kant, as incompatible with the world of the understanding. And above we have seen that the same held for Leibniz, insofar as the 'scientist' understands the world as if there was no freedom in it, while only the philosopher realizes that the truth of this understanding lies within the intuition of freedom itself.

While this problem has generally been grasped by means of the difference between reason and the understanding, Nietzsche has grasped it in the difference between the 'small reason' and the 'great reason'. For the small reason Nietzsche's statement above is the expression of an unreasonable hubris. But this judgement does not come about on account of any real question concerning Nietzsche's thought, but on account of the general impossibility of greatness. If everything can be referred back to a cause, if everything can thus be denied greatness, then greatness itself becomes impossible. The 'small reason' – that is, the simple representation of the world in front of an independent consciousness – is merely destructive. It pretends to be able to judge everything without being able either to create or to understand creation. This 'small reason', having assumed the reign over contemporary European thought, represents a cleverness without truth, bereft of life. What it calls real and concrete are merely judged facts without any intrinsic value. As the 'biological determinist', modern men might still have an intuition of freedom and the will, but can no longer entertain this intuition within the way that they understand themselves and the world.

From the perspective of the great human being, there is no idea here of megalomania. A Caesar, Plato, Leibniz, Newton, Napoleon, Goethe, Hegel or Nietzsche, for example, does not pride himself on his achievement, precisely because it appears as fate, i.e. according to the experience that one could not have done otherwise. Nietzsche, for example, does not pride himself on having found the truth, but experiences truth as 'speaking through him' (6/365). This truth can speak through him, because it has become in him 'flesh and genius' (6/365). Why it has done so is a different question, but one that cannot be meaningfully posed, insofar as the 'why' refers back to a possible cause, while fatalism as much as the intuition of freedom escapes the representation of the world in the image of causality.

While Napoleon thus does what he does, the philosophers

have no right to be individuals: we neither have a right to individual error, nor to hit on a truth individually. Rather, our thoughts, our values, our yes and no, our ifs and whethers, grow from out of us with the same necessity with which a tree grows its fruit. All of them related and in respect of each other. Witnesses of one will, one health, of one reign on earth and one sun. (5/248f)

CHAPTER 2

HISTORY AS SELF-CREATION

The product of the philosopher is his life.

We have learned that thinking for Nietzsche is much more than just being in possession of good ideas built up in a coherent fashion. Insofar as thinking is essentially related to one's being and, more concretely, to the living body, thinking, teaching and education generally have to be understood accordingly. While beliefs, opinions or ideas can be changed like one changes one's socks, true philosophical knowledge is something I do not only have, but which concerns my very being. On this point, too, Nietzsche returns to Plato, for whom the fact of knowledge is what characterizes the human being in its very existence. For the same reason the question of education lies at the heart of Plato's and Nietzsche's philosophy. In Plato's terms one can understand education as the care for the finitude of the human being. Knowledge is here not only the abstract knowledge that I have about certain things; rather that I have knowledge of the ideas is the reason why I can experience a world in the first place.

When we speak today of animal behaviour in terms of behaviourism, leading us to say that the antelope, for example, does not see a lion in order then to decide that she should run away, but reacts according to a simple and immediate stimulus–response mechanism, then this conviction is Platonic. From here we can see that we understand the animal to be bound to the present, while knowledge frees the human being and delivers it over to temporal duration. Only the human being sees, hears and touches a world insofar as the knowledge of ideas allows it to double up reality in order to see something *as* something. Thus, who I am and what I can do both depend on the question of knowledge. In the following we will thus elaborate the relation that our knowledge has to the questions of education and history. Having done so we will be in a position to understand the central teachings of Nietzsche, namely the thought of European history from the perspective of the *Death of God*, and his responses to this nihilism in the form of the doctrine of the *Eternal Return of the Same* and the understanding of the world as *Will to Power*.

i. THE WAY TO WISDOM: CAMEL, LION, CHILD

Plato and Nietzsche are equally in agreement on the claim that knowledge is not something given to me, ready-made, by a teacher. Rather knowledge is something I always already have implicitly within myself, while the task of teaching is to make it explicit, thereby realizing it in the literal sense of the word, i.e. making it a reality in my own existence. This is what Plato calls maieutic teaching, thereby comparing the teacher to a midwife, who merely facilitates the realization of the knowledge of the student. The education of its citizens is thus the highest task of the city state and it is itself a political task. We have just seen that Plato makes the distinction between animal and human existence on account of this fact of knowledge.

Yet, first of all, this knowledge is only implicit and therefore education is a task directed at the essence of the human being. To say this in other words, the human being *is* not free, it *becomes* free. Insofar as the human being is understood as free, this is because it can step over the immediate limits of that which is given. This stepping over we call *transcendence*. Yet this transcendence is not a mere attribute of humanity, but the result of practices, namely of education and political contestation. In other words, true freedom is given in that the essence of the human being is the task of humanity itself. Transcendence is then not only given in that the human being steps over the limits of the present, but in that, doing so, it steps over towards its own essence.

But stepping over towards its own essence means that the human being is not just what it is, but that it is given to itself only in its becoming. This insight lies at the root of both Nietzsche's demand to 'become the one that one is' and his claim regarding 'the infinite importance of our knowledge, our errors, of our habits and ways of life for all that is to come' (9/494). This statement stems from a first elaboration of the thought of the *Eternal Return of the Same*, which is to bring about a decision as to whether the human being will, after the death of God, become either animal or *Overhuman*. In the age of European Nihilism, where the human being is reduced to its economic existence, losing the insight into the ontological importance of knowledge in this broader sense, the Platonic interpretation of the human being as half animal and half divine becomes impossible.

This insight into the danger of contemporary life has influenced many thinkers of the twentieth century. Thus in a text called *Eye and Mind*, the French philosopher Maurice Merleau-Ponty argues that once our ideas of 'natural information processes' conceived on the

> model of human machines . . . were to extend their dominion over humanity and history . . . then, since man really becomes the *manipulandum* he takes himself to be, we enter into a cultural regimen where there is neither truth nor falsity concerning man and history, into a sleep, or a nightmare, from which there is no awakening. (Eye 122)

What Merleau-Ponty here owes to Nietzsche is the insight that what we take ourselves to be can as such become true. This might have been an error, but we have just heard about the 'infinite importance of . . . our errors . . . for all that is to come'. Knowledge is thus not just an objective observation of facts, but determines our future being. One of the greatest dangers of our age is hence identified by Nietzsche as the 'absence of a feeling for the importance of know-ledge' (7/542). And while we might today talk about such import-ance, this is generally reduced to the utility of economics, thereby missing completely the true meaning of education.

True education is, consequently, directed at becoming human and this becoming human is thus directed towards the care of its own essence, which makes it the properly political task. That is, the human being cannot be conceived of in isolation, but is always already in a community, and as the stepping over to its own essence can thus only be understood as the historical task of the human community, Nietzsche understands the reality of human freedom at once as the breeding of humankind and as 'great politics'. The human being thus never coincides with itself but finds itself in its collective future. Or, if it interprets its own existence as coinciding with itself, it will lose itself and become an 'animal'. The contestation of the question of what the human being should be and how it should live in community is then the highest political task and it is for this reason that the highest educators are also the guardians of the city. It is the participation in the contestation of these political questions on the market square, the *agora*, which decides on this becoming human, and whoever is excluded from this contestation is not seen as being human. Being excluded from the *agora* means being restricted to the *oikos*, that is to say, to household matters or what we today call the *economy*, a word directly derived from the Greek *oikos*.

We have already encountered the main difference between Plato and Nietzsche on this question of education and its ontological significance: while, for Plato, knowledge is an ideal possession of the memory of the soul, Nietzsche understands it as given in the history of the living body. That is to say that instincts, drives and habitual convictions are a historical memory having become flesh. These instincts and drives, making up parts of our knowledge, are the sedimentations of the beliefs and convictions of our ancestors, while thereby having become self-evident. Insofar as we think of drives and instincts nowadays as 'natural', what for Plato were philosophical questions have for us become 'facts of nature'.

But as soon as we take education as directed at the living body, it is not surprising that Nietzsche often addresses it under the title of *Zucht* and *Züchtung*: discipline and breeding. These conceptions have led to a lot of misunderstanding, as they first appear to us racist and essentially undemocratic. While there is no doubt that Nietzsche is explicitly undemocratic and argues consistently against the ideas of socialism, one should be careful not to conclude from this that he must of necessity be right wing or even a fascist. At the very least his text shows with clarity that his thought is neither anti-Semitic nor generally racist.

Modern democracy and socialism are doctrines arising from the Enlightenment, especially from Kantian humanism. Such humanism apportions equal value to each and every human being and teaches the equality of all human beings. It says that all human beings should have equal rights, because they essentially are equal in their being. Kant's humanism is therefore one which calls for all human beings to shed their dependence on authorities beyond that of universal reason. When he calls on us to 'dare to think' for ourselves, he gives rise to our conviction that everyone is capable of developing a maturity of judgement, so as to partake in the self-governance of the people. This humanism was developed at about the time of the French Revolution and the consequent Napoleonic wars, which promised to deliver Europe from the injustice of monarchy and the violent consequences of nationalism, and it has given rise to the various discourses on freedom and equality that have characterized European politics ever since.

So what could possibly be wrong with this humanism, considering especially that Nietzsche, being one of the first advocates of a united Europe, shares in the critique of nationalism? Indeed, Nietzsche's critique of socialism and democracy is not primarily directed against its doctrine of equal rights. The problem with humanism is rather that it claims an absolute value for every human existence. If all human beings are of such value, then this value must necessarily be absolutely independent from what an individual has done or could possibly do, and it is, equally, independent from history or any becoming. When Kant grounds human experience on the notion of a transcendental subjectivity, he withdraws this form of subjectivity not only from historical development, but from the notion of time generally. In short, a human subject conceived of as a universal form never changes and thereby founds the equality of all human beings, whatever their circumstances or actions.

But freedom, according to Plato and Nietzsche, is concrete only when it directs itself to the essence of the human being, which is to say that the free act aims at my very existence, rather than leaving it indifferent. But if the Kantian subject is just what it is, then it makes such freedom impossible. Such an interpretation makes the human being coincide with its essence and is thus, according to Nietzsche, nihilistic.

There are two points we need to consider: 1) Kant seems aware of this problem when writing in the *Critique of Judgement* that his philosophy throws up the incompatibility of theoretical and practical philosophy, that is to say, of our knowledge of the objective world, on the one hand, and our experience of freedom, on the other hand; 2) looking at Kant's moral philosophy, we find that a moral act should be judged on the merit of its intention alone, so as to eliminate all the adverse factors, the chances of luck or disaster, by means of which circumstances beyond our powers of action or reflection might have turned a good intention into an evil outcome. But this means taking an idealistic outlook on morality, subtracting from it the reality of moral action.

According to the Enlightenment, the human being is of an absolute worth. Whatever it does, this worth can be neither lost nor won. Political action as an essential action becomes impossible and history itself loses all meaning and direction. This ideology of humanism Nietzsche calls the ideology of the *Last Man*. We have already encountered this point in a quotation from the *Antichrist*, in which Nietzsche called the last man the one who 'is everything and knows not which way to turn' (AC 125). This is, then, the *last* man by his own decree, insofar as he has said that nothing can change in the form of human subjectivity, in that he has made himself independent of the torrent of historical time. It is true that we found in Leibniz a philosophy that understands action as a moral question, but we have seen that there action was itself understood as an ideal possession of the monad and that, consequently, time is seen merely as the sequence of moments by means of which my being unfolds itself in front of me and by means of which I take possession of myself, while this self and anything that belongs to it was, in truth, always already given.

We have suffered from not knowing where to go, precisely because we are already everything; in other words, because we cannot *become* anything, so that life, action and thought become more and more meaningless. If one is already born perfect then nothing essential is left to do while alive. Life itself thus becomes something indifferent. This is why Nietzsche calls this modernity the time of the *Last Man*, as he lacks in future and in promise. This *Last Man* coincides with himself, which is to say that he is without future and essentially lonely. And it is not difficult to see that, given its essence in pure thought – that is, in its conscious representation – this *Last Man* is himself becoming a fact.

Humanism portrays the human being as something ready-made; it has come today to see education as a simple process of stuffing information and transferable skills into the youth, so that it may prove itself in the economy. Even the university has today to subject itself to economic demands, be that with respect to the furthering of the local economy or with respect to winning the competition between national economies, while Nietzsche, in 'On the

Future of our Educational Institutions', argues that educational institutions, high schools and universities, should, on account of their essential political task, stand above and independent of the state.

The *Last Man* is becoming a fact, and a fact is something given clearly and distinctly, in the present. While it is something that 'has been made', it is not concerned with its past as it can be clearly understood from the present. Such a being is necessarily part of the world seen as mechanism, or, as we said above, of animals determined by Descartes as those beings that lack a soul. And indeed, while humanism said, on the one hand, that human beings are of an infinite worth, its scientific side says, on the other hand, that there is no essential difference between animals and human beings. Looking at behaviourism, genetic theory or the 'selfish gene', we can see that, being everything, the human being has already become nothing. This is not to say that modernity has not bred a certain kind of human being. Its values of objectivity, truthfulness, rationality, etc. have led to a homogenization of human existence, so that by feeling the same, seeing the same, experiencing the same and wanting the same things, the community is today stronger than ever and extending further than ever, up to that universal extension which we today call cosmopolitanism or even the 'Global Village'. But it has done so precisely by ignoring that this was its own doing; or, as Nietzsche says, we have bred the human being by accident. To educate consciously, on the other hand, means to make of the community a reality, which is to say, not as the sum total of identical particulars, but in terms of social difference: 'One might, by means of lucky inventions, educate the great individual in other and higher ways than it has been done hitherto by accident. Here are my hopes: the breeding of the outstanding human beings' (8/43).

The idea of breeding is nothing new, insofar as we can find it in the development of all culture. The *Genealogy of Morality* in particular brings out this point very clearly, namely that religion, the state, the various institutions, from schools and universities to the penal system, law courts and military installations are all engaged in bending human beings into a form. As Nietzsche says in this book: 'We moderns have inherited millennia of conscience-vivisection and animal-torture inflicted on ourselves: we have had most practice in it, are perhaps artists in the field . . .' Yet, more essentially, it is these practices which give rise to the human being's duration through time, to its memory and thus its historical existence, to transcendence and hence human freedom. The most essential of these breeding practices with respect to a fundamental account of truth are the Greek practices of rhetoric and the drive towards objectivity in the development of the sciences. Insofar as here, in juridical discourse and scientific practice, is developed a notion of truth as doing justice to things, they are effective in that they break down the narrow horizon of self-interest. The whole question of history thus comes down to asking ourselves which cultural means were necessary to breed an animal that can promise itself to the future, which is to say, can keep a promise even against its own inclinations, an animal with memory which can speak the truth.

Education, then, is for Nietzsche not simply a task to enlighten consciousness with abstract truths, but it is in the proper sense of the German word a *Bildung*, which is to say, a process of formation, a moulding process, or, as Nietzsche later calls it, the most essential form of breeding. In this respect he always seems to remain close to Plato's idea of a great politics as outlined most essentially in the *Laws*. We have found many points on which Nietzsche's thought agrees with Plato's and this might be called the most essential one, namely that the whole aim of philosophy is that of a *paideia*, which is to say, an education in the most essential sense of forming the human being with respect to the formation of a political society. Such education is then the most essential task of the political community, and, insofar as the formation of the state is equally at stake in it, such education has to remain independent from any existing state.

The first and foremost task of education is to breed an animal that can promise itself, that is, one which exists through time, and which thus does not coincide with itself as a fact does, but which finds its essence in the future. And it is precisely insofar as its essence lies in the future, that we do not find within the human being much that is fixed: 'The new reformer sees human beings as clay. By means of time and institutions just about anything can be built into them, one can turn them into animals or angels. There is hardly anything solid. "Reformation of humankind!" ' (8/355)

But it would be a mistake to see an essential difference here between the metaphysical task of the formation of the human being, on the one hand, and the everyday behaviour of human beings, on the other. One of the radical changes of the perspective of the body on our understanding of philosophy is that it opens up the perspective of the everyday. The philosopher no longer lives in his ivory tower, from which he can survey the grand problems of humankind, in order to judge on the great questions of freedom, divine existence and immortality. Instead this notion of education has to take into account the smallest differences in the life of human beings. We have seen one example already: while Plato can denounce the worldliness of the sophists as being merely concerned with gaining money by rhetorical means, Nietzsche discerned in these very practices the origin of our will to truth. Equally he insists that we have to pay attention to the smallest things:

> All habitualization [e.g. to specific food, coffee, for example, or a specific time management] finally leads to the breeding of a specific kind of human beings. Therefore: look at your life! Examine the smallest things. . . . Do they belong to your type, to your purpose? (9/525)

Looking at history we can say, then, that any age to which we attach the idea of greatness must show signs of an intensified practice of breeding, where the greatness of these achievements can be measured with respect to the freedom of the human being. While we might be thinking that today the human being is more free than it had been in the age of the Greek city states, which economically relied on slavery, we have already seen that freedom is not reducible to the question of being able to make whatever indifferent decisions in consciousness, but requires a concrete realization of oneself built on a multitude of perspectives on the world, the outcome of which is a realization that life was, can and will be otherwise than it presents itself to me in the immediate necessity of my factual present. 'Wherever we find enduring greatness, we can discern a diligent practice of breeding, e.g. with the Greeks', Nietzsche says, and wonders, 'How was it possible for so many of them to achieve freedom?' (8/46).

Such an age can throw its shadows over many millennia of history and that is precisely what the Greek age has done. The Greek age is not only the cradle of European culture, it has not only determined all the ideas we entertain concerning metaphysics, theology, morality, the arts and culture, and human existence generally; it is not only that we still speak Greek when we say *philosophy, technology* or *economy*, but any idea of real creation seems possible only by means of returning to the Greek soil of thinking, so much so that Alfred North Whitehead (1861–1947), a famous English philosopher, has said that all of philosophy is but a footnote to Plato. Two of Nietzsche's main examples are those of the Renaissance, which as one of the greatest ages of recent history could create only by understanding itself as a *rebirth* of the Greek age, without copying it, and that of German philosophy, whose greatness he sees in rediscovering the ancient Greek soil. Another example is our notion of a humanistic education, which is always and at the same time a classical education. This is not to say that we need to be filled with lots of data about the Greek age, but rather, as Karl Jaspers says, following Nietzsche: without a classical education, without having encountered the Greek age, we forget all too easily that life can be otherwise than it is and thus we easily sink into the conviction that everything is just as it can be, that life is but a collection of facts binding me to the prison of the present.

In this sense the creative side of education is always bound to a repetition of the past. And from this notion of repetition stem the contradictions of Nietzsche's view on history: on the one hand, he sees European history as a progressive decline from ancient Greece to the present, while, on the other, it is only this history, as he says, that has made the human being interesting; on the one hand, he admires the tragic age of the Greeks while, on the other, his own thought stands or falls by its success in overturning Platonism, which is to say, the most significant part of the breeding practices which, over the course of the last two millennia, have given rise to the beings that we are ourselves. It is thus this active taking over of my own being in education that realizes history as the 'phylogenesis' of the different types of historical human existence. The aim of education consists in this realization and in the 'speeding up' of the whole process: 'The transformation of the human being first needs millennia for the formation of a type, then generations: finally one human being moves during its life through a number of individual types' (9/547).

And yet, insofar as we are talking about the development of the body, we are confronted with two conclusions. The first concerns the uninterrupted nature of the historical presence in the morphology of the body. This is, as we will see, similar to the living memory of Hegel's world spirit, which can take possession of itself only insofar as and as long as it is in possession of its history. If some rungs of the ladder were to be lost, the aim of education would withdraw from reach.

> Just take the Greeks away, including their philosophy and art: which ladder are you going to use to climb towards education? In the attempt to climb the ladder without any help, your learnedness may . . . sit on your neck as an unhelpful ballast, rather than inspiring you and pulling you upwards. (1/733)

The second consequence concerns the relation between that which changes and that which is changed. If we think of the history of the species in terms of natural selection, as we can approach it since Darwin, then we have, on the one hand, the chance mutations of genes which change the individuals of the species and, on the other hand, the experiences of these individuals, selecting positive from negative mutations. These two levels are separated like a transcendental form from its empirical content, insofar as experience has no influence in whatever sense on the level of mutation. That is to say, experience is here understood as merely passive. With Hegel and Nietzsche, on the contrary, we are speaking about an inheritance of experience itself.

Of course the idea of breeding domesticated animals, like dogs, cats or cows, already allows for such an idea, but here the breeder stands to the bred like God stands to the human being, which is to say, action and passion are infinitely separated, so that the act of breeding can still be conceived according to our general idea of an action as derived from conscious deliberation, creating an image of the aim of breeding and a consequent engagement of experience in the actual act of breeding. But, if human culture is understood as breeding, if self-conscious, responsible and rational thinking is itself seen as arising from these acts of education, then the difference between action and passion, between representation and experience breaks down and we are engaged in the unified idea of history, of the history of human emotion, sensibility, thought, art, science, etc.

That this self-creation of the human being has to be understood as art means that the bred and the breeding fall into one. Consequently, we cannot understand this action as a conscious process motivated by an ideal image. This is why Nietzsche says that we have failed to assume responsibility for this action, precisely because we have made it invisible by, first, attributing it to God, and, second, attributing it to a mechanical and objective process of nature. Understanding it in the proper sense of art as *techne*, on the other hand, it can be conceived only as experimentation.

> Those natural processes in the breeding of the human being, which have hitherto been practised incredibly slowly and clumsily, could be taken over by human beings: and the old bearishness of races, of racial wars, the fever of nationalism and personal jealousies could, at least in experiments, be condensed to a short duration. (9/547)

In this quotation we find the two key points from above, namely the idea of how we can think of such a process as experimentation and the positive aims followed by such experimentation. This experimentation is thus not without a telos, but this is not to be understood as a positive image, enumerating predicates of an ideal object. Instead Nietzsche sees it as derived from the historical situation and its illnesses. As a consequence of this, Nietzsche calls educational institutions 'workshops in the struggle against the present' (7/262). The notion of these workshops combines the idea of philosophy as a *techne* and its essence as experimentation.

We have found many reasons why Nietzsche's teachings may not be clear and distinct. First, because, as teachings, they are supposed to be movements and therefore not given in the present. Second, they are conceived from the position of the 'great reason', that is, the living body, in such a way that I who have the thought am at the same time that what I am thinking, which is to say that I cannot take a theoretical distance from it. Third, the style of presentation, its rhetoric, cannot be subtracted from its truth – that is, its form is not indifferent to its content. Fourth, philosophical thinking tries to understand a life-world which itself is not simple. Consequently truth itself is not simple and the measure of wisdom is, for Nietzsche, how much truth one can incorporate, given that this demands of the thinker the ability to give rise to many contradictory modes of thinking. Fifth, the teacher is herself not a divine being who has thoughts to pass on, but is herself always directed both to herself and to the public. As far as Nietzsche speaks of knowledge as the inner strife within the thinker, these two sides clarify that knowledge is not apart from darkness and shadow. Indeed, knowledge has to be unearthed from darkness and it always remains drawn to it. Consequently Nietzsche can say that the product of the philosopher is his life (7/712) and that his writings are fundamentally only about himself (6/319).

And who is Nietzsche? 'I am originally and from my first beginnings, drawing [*ziehend*], attracting [*heranziehend*], pulling upwards [*hinaufziehend*], a grower [*Zieher*], breeder [*Züchter*], disciplinarian [*Zuchtmeister*], who told himself once for good reasons: "become the one who you are!" ' (4/295). You can see from the German originals that all these words belong to one family, which Nietzsche here alludes to in order to show their essential relation within the idea of education. This educator, liberating us from our imprisonment in the 'small reason' of consciousness is thus at the same time liberating himself, which is the reason why we see Zarathustra, the teacher of the *Eternal Return of the Same* and the *Overhuman*, constantly striving with the explication of these teachings as determining him who teaches them.

But we need not restrict ourselves to examples from Nietzsche's text, considering that we can take the structure of his whole work as exemplifying his notion of education. Thus one can easily identify three phases within Nietzsche's work: the early writings from the 1870s, including 'The Birth of Tragedy'; the middle period extending from the late 1870s to the mid 1880s; and the last period, beginning with *Thus Spake Zarathustra*. The first of these 'phases' is characterized by the thinker who admires the Greeks, who reveres Wagner and who sees himself as the pupil of Schopenhauer. This is the time that Nietzsche later describes in terms of a diligence of learning and obedience, as collecting within oneself all that is worthy of admiration despite the contradictoriness and tension between the various things learned (11/159). This beginning of education is thus characterized by bearing all the great weight of the tradition on one's shoulders. In the first of Zarathustra's speeches, 'Of the Three Metamorphoses', Nietzsche names this stage in the following way: ' "What is heavy?" asks the weight-bearing spirit, thus it kneels down like the camel and wants to be well laden' (Z 54).

As Nietzsche points out in the early lectures 'On the Future of our Educational Institutions', all true education is fundamentally opposed to the modern ideas of education, which often try to achieve an equivalence between teacher and student, wishing to grant to the latter the status of a customer, who might choose what to learn and what not to learn (1/733). All true *Bildung* begins with submission to the tradition and its order, with an obedience that becomes tolerable by the adulation of the greatness of the past on the part of the student. The true measure of the intellect is thus acquired here as the test of how much truth a spirit can bear and bring to a strife within herself without despairing (6/259). As we will see later, this measure is not simply one of being able to judge many things, but it concerns the ground-laying for the development of the will.

What we nowadays call a 'critical education', on the other hand, where the student is forced to show her ability by immediately starting to criticize whatever she is presented with, mostly before even having understood what the work criticized is about, lays the ground for a resentful spirit. This cannot find any value in its critique, because from the start the criticized does not seem to be of much value and is unable to resist even the most obvious critique. Nietzsche often links this notion of a critical education to the rise of journalism, and one needs only to view the recent series of BBC television programmes on Nietzsche, Heidegger and Sartre (*Human, All Too Human*, first broadcast in 1999) to see what he meant. Here the philosophy of all these thinkers is easily understood and as easily criticized and the viewer wonders afterwards why these men would have been called 'great philosophers', considering that 'everyone' could have had these thoughts, while 'everyone' would not have gone on to write these down, because 'everyone' could quickly see why they were quite wrong. In this way the student feels she can master these philosophers, but at the same time she realizes that there is nothing to be gained by studying the history of the human being, that in herself she is nothing.

It is only when the camel has first loaded itself with the weight of more than 2,500 years of historical achievement, only once it admires these and seems to be bound to reverence that it can criticize with any weight behind this criticism. And not even because it now knows so much about it, not because it has infinite bounds of information at its command, but because it now has to 'break its own worshipping heart' (11/159). The time of the lion is thus the time of the desert, where the spirit breaks all that it has revered, but without being capable of putting anything in its place. The lion can thus not criticize on account of judgement; rather it has to judge that everything that has been is worthy of destruction. 'To create new values – even the lion is incapable of that: but to create freedom for new creation – that the might of the lion can do' (Z 55).

Looking at the writings of Nietzsche that fall into this second period, we can see more clearly what he means. *Human, All too Human, The Dawn* and, if to a lesser degree, *The Gay Science*, seem to carry through an intention of pure destruction, of a critique in the form of an absolute scepticism, excelling any such attempt in the history of philosophy. All these works are composed in a fragmentary style, with the meanings of various fragments striving against each other. These works do not seem to destroy this or that philosophical position, in order to arrive at a true judgement, but they make any idea of a simple truth incredible. And yet, after reading these works the reader recognizes that this is not an exercise in wanton destruction, but that the notion of the will undergoes certain mutations, thereby achieving a meaning even though this never coalesces into a systematic standpoint.

The original last lines of *The Gay Science* are then already giving expression to Nietzsche's realization that he is now in a position to move further, announcing in § 341 the teaching of *Eternal Recurrence* and in § 342 the arrival of Zarathustra. Considering that we generally tend to understand education as issuing in the mature, grown-up spirit, which has gained the recognition of its independent judgement, this last metamorphosis might come as a surprise. Following Plato, Leibniz and others in the claim that the human spirit cannot move from scientific knowledge to true, philosophical knowledge by increments of learning, Nietzsche speaks of this third step in terms of a great decision, namely whether the spirit is capable of affirmation, which is to say, of creation.

The proper philosophical attitude is, then, not likened to the mature judge presiding in the courtroom of wisdom, but to the child who creates from the position of a newly acquired innocence. 'The child is innocence and forgetfulness, a new beginning, playing, a self-propelling wheel, a first motion, a sacred yes' (Z 55). At the end of these metamorphoses thus stands a new beginning, the child as the being that does not look back to the past but that is given in its openness to the future, that is thus not suffering from determinism in the great mechanical world, but that is open to its fate. The time of history given through the prevalence of the future is here subverting the idea we have concerning the soil that we live upon: 'What of fatherland! Our helm wants to fare *away*, out to where our *children's land* is' (Z 231).

It is not that Nietzsche knew from the outset about this necessity of education and that he consequently produced these three phases over the course of his work. It is not that he consciously planned out his life to put it into practice. Rather it is here at the time of the *Zarathustra* that he realizes that his experiment concerning the embodiment of history has come together into one development, allowing him to assume the position of the teacher. But, up to this moment everything that he had done could have still revealed itself as that which every experimenter constantly dreads, namely a failure. As the philosopher has only one life, for him there is only one experiment, which explains Nietzsche's euphoria while writing the *Zarathustra* as well as the decision taken by him at this time, namely that he would embark on the writing of his ultimate work, defining his life.

This final work exists only as a sequence of titles and plans written during the last five years of his sane existence. It is variously called *The Will to Power*, *The Innocence of Becoming* or *The Revaluation of all Values*, though there are other titles besides these. In a few of these plans the title *The Antichrist* exists as the title of an introductory first chapter, supposed to build the critical step over which one could move, out of Platonic metaphysics, towards a new Nietzschean thought. In the end, Nietzsche publishes a book called *The Antichrist*, which one might perfectly see as the introduction to such a work, while the outline of a new thought never comes to pass. This elated state of a well-earned innocence hence only exists in the form of the *Zarathustra*.

Still, now that Nietzsche has produced himself as this experiment in which the human being discovers the historical reality of its embodied thought, now that we have experienced the radical truth of historical becoming, now that we have seen how one can attempt to liberate oneself from the imprisonment of thought in abstract consciousness, now that the experiment 'Nietzsche' has become an integral part of our phylogenesis, that is, of our fate, we no longer need to concern ourselves with Nietzsche or his life, but with those things for the sake of which he existed (8/553).

ii.   THE DISCOVERY OF HISTORY IN HEGEL

We Germans are Hegelians, even if there never had been any Hegel, insofar as we (in opposition to the Latins) instinctively grant a deeper sense and a richer value to becoming than to that which 'is'. – We hardly believe in the justification of the word 'being'.

Nietzsche's indebtedness to Hegel has mostly been overlooked, often because he was seen as a pupil of Schopenhauer, who nurtured a deep hatred for Hegel. And yet Nietzsche's judgement on this hatred is quite uncompromising: 'with his unintelligent rage against Hegel [Schopenhauer] succeeded in disconnecting the entire last generation of Germans from German culture, which culture was, all things considered, a high point and divinatory refinement of the *historical sense* . . .' (BGE 204). Without wanting to diminish the influence of Schopenhauer on Nietzsche's thought, it is still the case that Hegel's fundamental idea of a speculative dialectics, in which all development is understood by a process of recognizing oneself in that which is other, was also Nietzsche's entry into philosophy:

> When I was just 12 years old, I thought of a wondrous Three-Oneness: namely God-Father, God-Son and God-Devil. My syllogism was that God, thinking himself, created the second person of the Godhead: but that in order to be able to think himself, he had to think, that is, create, his antithesis. – With this thought I began to philosophize. (11/253)

This is a typically Hegelian thought in that it stipulates that God can only be himself by means of the contradiction of his opposite, and that he can only be by being recognized by this other. Thus at the tender age of 12 years, long before reading Schopenhauer, Nietzsche already had an insight into the truth of the Hegelian principle of the dialectic of the real, according to which 'contradiction moves the world, all things are in that they are essentially self-contradictory'.

But what is a 'dialectic of the real'? The word 'dialectic' derives from the Greek *dia* and *lexis*, and literally means 'through the tongue'. Thus Plato argued that the truth is not given in abstract thought, but that it can only be reached 'through the tongue', which is to say, by means of contradiction in dialogue. One thus has to discuss matters with others to find the truth, while on one's own one will never reach a truth. But this is not only to say that there have to be at least two human beings speaking to each other for there to be any insight into the truth. What immediately follows from the dialectical method of thinking is that I cannot really ignore the means by which I get to know something with respect to the knowledge that I have finally arrived at.

The word method, in turn, derives from the Greek *met'hodos*, speaking of 'the path by means of which' I can reach a result. This method can thus not be ignored as it is an integral part of the truth that I have found. And yet, insofar as this method describes a movement, a becoming of thought, it cannot be represented in the form of a result. Here we can see a first dimension of the thought of history: to understand something historically is not only to compare it to its contemporary context, to where it comes from and where it has led to. Rather it is to understand its movement as something real. This is why philosophy cannot simply trade in ideas, conceived as clear and distinct, and it is for the same reason that there are no 'naked' facts in the world of history. As Hegel says, what is important to philosophy is the path through which the result was reached, while 'the bare result is the corpse which has left the guiding tendency behind it' (PoS 3).

But what holds for my thinking certainly also holds for myself. Human life in its historical concretion cannot be understood as a sum total of facts or data and the true philosophical science thus has to attempt to grasp the movement of life itself if it then wants to understand human reality. This is because the human being cannot be grasped insofar as it simply *is*, but insofar as it *acts*. 'The true being of man is his action', as Hegel says. Thus, insofar as I attempt to understand the idea of thinking or knowing, I will have to grasp these too as actions. This is precisely what Nietzsche does in the early essay 'On Truth and Lying in a Non-Moral Sense', namely to criticize our whole conception of action itself insofar as we think of it as consisting in three parts, namely deliberation, decision and 'actual' action. Our whole morality depends on the idea that I first think about the right act, that I then decide to act on this insight and that I then act. But these are three actions, as Nietzsche says. Our whole philosophy, morality and political thought have suffered from this misunderstanding of the temporal reality of thinking, and they have consequently attempted to grasp human reality from the perspective of the 'naked corpse'.

To ignore the effective nature of history is, then, to ignore life and to stultify it, for which reason Nietzsche stresses the unity of these two themes when criticizing the idiosyncrasies of the philosophers. What these have in common is

> their lack of historical sense, their hatred of the very idea of becoming, their Egypticism. They think they are doing a thing an *honour* when they dehistoricize it, . . . when they make a mummy out of it. All that philosophers have been handling for thousands of years is conceptual mummies; nothing real has ever left their hands alive. (TI 16)

The discovery of history in Hegel, the realization that any actuality is derived from human acts, thus first allows us to look at the world from the perspective of life, where one had previously looked down onto the world, so to speak, from the imagined perspective of a god. It is this perspective of life that Nietzsche tries more and more to discover and to claim for philosophical thinking. Thus when wondering about the truth of the modern sciences, he does not do so from any abstract perspective but, as he says, from the perspective of life. It is, in the end, we human beings who ask questions and these questions have an interested perspective. They try to help us understand the world, to find our place in it and to further our activity in the world. To forget this interested perspective means for Nietzsche equally to forget any concrete notion of truth.

This point becomes immediately clear when considering the title of Nietzsche's essay on history, namely 'On the Advantages and Disadvantages of History for Life', and its first line, a quotation from Goethe: 'Moreover I hate everything which merely instructs me without increasing or directly quickening my activity'. Nietzsche here makes clear that a questioning of history in what we call the 'objective' or scientific mode is not only superfluous and boring, but also wrong. Such a mode implies a perspectiveless perspective, which is self-contradictory, and it thus bases its claims on nothing. We could make this point with the words of the twentieth-century philosopher Otto Neurath (1882–1945), when he asks whether the truths of our sciences are truths even for 'seventeen-legged Martians who never eat and enjoy their decay'. Such a question is as absurd as it sounds and shows the profound mistake of the assumption of an 'uninterested' perspective. When one speaks of a perspectivism in Nietzsche's works, one should never forget that this is not simply to say that we should give credence to various ideas of the world, but that we should look at existence from the perspective of life.

We have seen this point a few times: to make fact one's idol means to become an advocate of the devil; that is, to look at life from the uninterested perspective of death. Life, on the other hand, is always on the move, but that is to say that its being is not something present, factual, but always an action, a changing this into that, which is what Hegel calls negation. Hegel gives a good example of this insight when making fun of common sense in the *Phenomenology of Spirit*. He asks 'What is the truth of the apple?' Common sense begins to list its attributes, that is, describes its factual being, while Hegel retorts that even the animals are more intelligent: instead of merely gazing at the apple, they fall to it and eat it up. And, indeed, the truth of the apple is to be eaten.

But this is to say that the truth of the apple is not independent from the world and thus not to be found in its 'objective' existence. And this does not only hold for the apple, but is equally true of consciousness. The truth of my being is not simply given and to be known, but it exists in my actions. If that is the case, then it becomes clear that the truth of these actions is not necessarily something I do know or even can know. We have attempted above to understand the dialectic of the real, having said that here at least two tongues contradict each other; which is to say, speak against each other. But, who does speak when I open my mouth? Is it really 'my' consciousness? I, obviously, speak in a language that I have not invented and I often speak about things in a way that I have heard from others. 'I' read books and newspapers, watch television and listen to my teachers, and all these communications form my opinions and my thought generally. We might as well say that mostly we speak with the voices of others – and these are not even concrete others, but just about 'anyone'. Even if, without knowing, I begin repeating things that I have heard from others, these others have not invented these things either. It is for these reasons that we generally understand each other remarkably well.

At the same time we often have the experience that we have difficulty saying what we want to say, while also often realizing only after we have said something what it was that we wanted to say.

Insofar as language is the medium in which we speak and insofar as it has a historical depth – that is, insofar as language speaks to me from the past as well as from my own age – Hegel demonstrates that truth lies not in conscious representation, but in language. Dialectics thus refers not only to the community of human beings, but also to the insight that consciousness is not the locus of truth. 'Language ... is the more truthful', Hegel says: 'in it, we ourselves directly refute what we *mean* to say' (PoS 60).

This, as we said, seems already to have been the case for Plato. And yet, for him the dialectic seems to have been merely a tool, a method of gaining knowledge, while Hegel spoke of a 'dialectic of the real'. If my actions are my true being, what then is the real world and what is it that here contradicts each other? The real world is full of things: courtrooms, police stations, parliaments, museums, dogs, schools, universities, buildings of all kinds, football grounds, motorways, libraries, cows, parks, banks, supermarkets, submarines, planes, etc., etc. What all these things have in common is that they are historical sedimentations of human actions. When I think of myself as an individual subject, this is dependent on the development of Roman property law. When I think of myself as a student, this depends on Plato having founded the first Academy and on all those who have kept it alive during the following 2,400 years. When I think of myself as a soldier, this depends on the history of European warfare. One could give an infinite string of various examples here.

What is important for Hegel is to realize that it is not only that the individual consciousness has to be thought from out of the perspective of a 'collective' which might contradict me, but that it is the whole world that exists in and through such contradiction. In it a feudal law contradicts its capitalist economy, military concerns contradict democratic institutions, the ideologies of the middle classes contradict the interests of the working class, nature contradicts culture, my knowledge of the world is contradicted by the reality of this world, etc., etc., which is also to say that none of these are just what they are, but are given in and through these contradictions. And, as contradiction is an act which 'moves through time', these contradictions cannot be truly conceived in their present state, but are motivated by history. Consequently, I am my past. This is what it means to say that 'contradictions move the world'.

In short, the world is a human world and when 'I' speak, the whole world speaks though my mouth. The truth of consciousness is thus equally given in the dimension of this historical world. The totality of these relations between myself, the other human beings and the world of all 'objects' Hegel calls *spirit*. The *Phenomenology of Spirit* is thus an account of the reality of human existence in the torrent of history; it is the attempt to understand my own reality as given to me in its historical concretion. Hegel thus uses the word 'spirit' as we might speak of the 'spirit of the 1920s' and the whole of history is understood by him as the sequence of these spirits, from the 'Greek spirit' via the 'Roman spirit' to the 'spirit of modernity'. But to say that I am my past insofar as I act, therefore directing myself to the future, is also to say that I do not learn about history for reasons of pure curiosity or to achieve 'objective' knowledge. Rather, I am myself in an authentic sense only on account of such a concrete historical memory. Or, it is only by knowing and being my past that I can act in any meaningful sense, and it is here that Nietzsche sees the possibility of understanding the world from the perspective of life.

The past is thus present everywhere: it is the presence of artworks, law courts, police stations, architecture, language, etc. In this sense I recollect my own existence from everywhere in the world, I recognize my being in actions which are directed towards such institutions and these actions are not conceived of from the perspective of a neutral consciousness. As we can see in the notion of spirit as the all-encompassing reality of thought and being, the individual consciousness itself is not in possession of its truth. It is always running ahead of what it knows and can develop precisely because it does not know, i.e. because it never coincides with itself. When Hegel speaks of master and slave, for example, the slave consciousness is a consciousness which does not know that it is such. Insofar as it still is a logical dialectic that governs its development, Hegel has discovered a thought that is not conscious, but embodied in the world itself. This point already followed from us having said that deliberation, decision and 'action' are three different forms of actions. Consciousness can only deal with representations, which is to say, with present structures, while the bigger part of thinking does not allow for this form: 'Man', as Nietzsche concludes from here, 'like every other being, thinks continually without knowing it; the thinking that rises to *consciousness* is only the smallest part of all this –' (GS 299).

But the attempt to recollect my own existence from the world is often not very successful. Instead I experience the world as unjust, as alien to my wishes. Hegel thus sees the totality of history as a history of alienation. This is to say that contradiction is what defines me in the sense of some impossibility of action. The Hegelian idea of history is not that of an infinite horizon of a natural history within which we find something like a human history. Instead, history is our history and as such it has a beginning and an end. Our history, as we often say, begins in the classical Greek age. If that is so, there must be a reason for it and this reason Hegel explains by arguing that at the beginning of history there was no contradiction. This is what he calls the beautiful ethical life of the Greeks. Like Nietzsche, he sees this age as the age of art, which means that we should be able to find our evidence for the beginning of history in art. Hegel finds it in Sophocles' famous tragic play *Antigone*.

We have no space here to go into this argument in any detail, so I will just state the main points. The original state, for Hegel, is one of harmony. Human law – that is, the political realm – exists in harmony with divine law, which is the law of family life: woman lives in harmony with man. The play *Antigone* then describes how this harmony breaks apart by mere accident, in that both human law and divine law claim the corpse of Antigone's brother. This breaking apart issues in a series of contradictions, as we said, between the individual and the state, between masters and slaves, between good and evil, between my knowledge and the world, between what is the case and what should be the case. The world and life itself suddenly appear unjustified and the human being turns away from this life. One begins to wonder if there is any being that could make sense of this world and if even God, had he just known about the invention of the big cannon, would have created this world. These contradictions move the European human being through its history.

But the notion of alienation says at the same time that I misrecognize myself, my thought and my actions, or that I do not know what I am doing and thinking. For that reason even philosophy appears as this immense contradiction in which everyone criticizes everyone else. The Enlightenment thinkers from Descartes to Kant, for example, tend to enter the arena with a feeling of superiority, declaring that 'everyone up to now has got it all wrong, while I will now tell you how to get it right'; or that 'there has not yet been any metaphysics worth that name, while I will now write its prolegomena'. At the same time they lay claim to such originality by discounting the influence of the philosophic tradition on their thinking. Of course, there are differences and many of these philosophers have a high regard for the great names of the tradition, or even legitimate, as Leibnitz does, a partial return to Plato, but generally speaking it seems that for these thinkers a philosophy is a system of thought that can be measured against other such systems in terms of its correspondence with reality. But that presupposes that one already experiences thought as being separated from this reality. Representational thinking is thus itself just one expression of alienation. Such alienation ends in the conviction that thought cannot capture the truth, that so many philosophers have tried and still there is no agreement. And even if one would, finally, stumble upon the truth and come up with a perfect system of thought, precisely because it would only be a correct image in thought, it would not change anything about the world.

With Hegel, on the other hand, all this changes and philosophy stops being 'original'. Instead of proclaiming that one need once more start afresh, Hegel finds the truth of philosophy in the reality of its historical becoming. To say this in simpler words, instead of finding reasons for which all systems of philosophy hitherto have been wrong, for Hegel they are all true expressions of the spirit of their days. Speaking of Plato, Descartes or Kant is not to find agreements and disagreements, shared ideas and possible corrections, but it is to understand them as expressions of the truth of their existence in the world.

Since Hegel the Germans have made a distinction between the words *Historie* and *Geschichte*, both of which are mostly translated as 'history'. The study of *Historie* is more or less what we know as history, namely to give an account of historical facts in their context and development. Thus one discerns the influence of battles, changes of rulers and forms of government, etc. in order to follow the course of history. In such investigations one might also look at a 'history of ideas', which discerns these as various beliefs and convictions appearing in the course of history. *Geschichte*, on the other hand, might be translated as *effective history*. Here history is not an object we can look at, but the reality of the becoming that has made us who we are and our social reality what it is.

The *Phenomenology of Spirit*, for example, provides something like a history of the experience of consciousness, but this is not strictly 'chronological' and does not follow the surface phenomena of history as we might find them in a history book. Rather it follows the essential changes that characterize the development of our way of thinking, of the arts, philosophical thought, culture, etc. In such an account of the effective becoming of historical truth, one might say, everything is true and it is the task of the philosopher to determine the significance of any such truth. Indeed, insofar as the whole historical world speaks through me, one could hardly conceive of the possibility of saying something 'wrong'. When Nietzsche says that 'I am all the names of history', or

> when I speak of Plato, Pascal, Spinoza and Goethe, then I am aware that their blood flows within mine – I am proud about saying the truth about them – the family is good enough, not being in need of fabulation or dissimulation; and thus I stand towards all that has been, I am proud of humanity, and proud especially in unconditioned truthfulness (9/585)

then it is this idea of an effective history that he has in mind. Knowing history is then nothing else but the attempt at knowing oneself.

The ideal of knowing history is to be able to affirm life, to say yes to it. Hegel thus demonstrates that all ills of history, from war and exploitation to death and destruction, while not seeming to have any intrinsic sense, can be understood as meaningful once looked at from the perspective of history, which he equally calls 'absolute life' or 'absolute spirit'. When he says of the latter that it is 'absolute knowing', this does not mean that it knows everything, being able to win any 'Who Wants to be a Millionaire?' show, but that its knowledge makes it one with its world, that it sees itself in the world and the world in its own existence – in short, that it can say yes to the whole world and to itself. The highest aspiration of philosophy is, for Hegel, captured in the famous sentence of the *Philosophy of Right*, namely: 'the real is rational and the rational is real', which is to say that 'the world is how it ought to be and what ought to be is'.

In this sense history is able to account for our understanding of the world without making it dependent on a true world of perfection bestowing meaning onto this world of imperfection. While philosophy since Plato has understood truth as throwing light onto this world from beyond this world – whether this be the ideas in heaven, the Christian paradise, the immortal soul in its union with God, or even the absolute form of subjectivity – Hegel accounts for the absolute as arising from this world of life itself. This is why the book is called the *Phenomenology of Spirit*. While traditional philosophy accounted for truth in the sense of something outside the world which appeared in the world, a phenomenon, according to its original Greek meaning, is something that shines through and by itself. Hegel expresses this idea that even the absolute is something belonging to the world of history in the form of a relatively inconspicuous sentence: that 'the supersensible is appearance *qua* appearance' (PoS 89). What Hegel means is that there is nothing which would give meaning to the world without itself being a part of it. Rather, the world is understood as the temporal, that is, historical constitution of its own meaning; it gives rise to the absolute from within itself.

This point is more radical than it might at first appear. When Descartes speaks of reason as the natural light, meaning that it is God-given and able to grant us truth precisely because it does not depend on this ephemeral world of becoming; when Kant speaks of the transcendental and thus pure notion of thought, unsullied by experience, these philosophies generally try to show that the rules of thought and its concepts are absolutes, which can thus be applied to a world in which everything seems to be in motion. By means of this rationality one might measure reality as one measures motion through a chronometer. That is to say, in the same way as the measurement of time is to be indifferent to whatever happens in it, the system of concepts is equally independent from what it is used to describe. This is the division that Plato set up between the world of motion and the world of truth: only insofar as the latter does not change at all can it be used to understand the world of constant change. Hegel, on the contrary, here argues that thought itself, reason and logic, depend on their historical becoming, that there thus is, similar to the idea of the evolution of the species, an 'evolution' of thought and concepts. Or, rather, it is the other way round: we first need to grasp the evolution of thought in order even to conceive of an evolution of the species. It is this originary nature of philosophical thinking which Nietzsche has in mind when reflecting on the astonishing stroke of *Hegel*, who struck right through all our logical habits when he dared to teach that species concepts develop *out of each other*. With this proposition the minds of Europe were preformed for the last great scientific movement, Darwinism – for without Hegel there could have been no Darwin. (GS 305)

With this notion of a historical development of thought and reason itself, Hegel and Nietzsche separated philosophy most radically from its Platonic heritage. There are no eternal truths, values, concepts, forms or souls, as Nietzsche says. From the perspective of history all concepts are themselves created and still in the process of their creation. From here Nietzsche concludes that the most universal concepts are equally the oldest and the most erroneous. 'Being', 'substance' and the 'unconditioned', 'equality', 'thing': these are all simplifications stemming from the earliest times of human development, from a time in which consciousness was still blunt, simple and, as Nietzsche says, not even on a par with that of animals (*untertierisch*) (11/613). While the philosophers have only handled 'conceptual mummies', have tried to understand the world of life by means of dead, eternal ideas, Hegel has put an end to this by means of the history of thought as the expression of absolute life.

With Hegel, not only Darwin becomes possible, but also the *Death of God*, which draws after it the downfall of all these simplifications. The historical sense, which Nietzsche also calls the sixth sense, is a refinement of human sensibility of which Plato and the whole of philosophy had no idea (11/254): 'We are the first aristocrats in the history of the human spirit – the historical sense begins with us' (9/642). Hegel has thus given us the ability to look at the world from the perspective of life, precisely by having discovered effective history. 'What separates us equally from Kant as from Plato and Leibniz: we believe in becoming also within thought, we are historical through and through. This is the great reversal. Lamarck and Hegel . . .' (11/442).

iii. NIETZSCHE VERSUS HEGEL

We have said that with Nietzsche history becomes the sole content of philosophy, thereby implying that this does not hold of Hegel. The first question bringing us closer to this point would be how

Hegel was able to see what nobody else had seen before him, namely that the world of human existence can be justified from the position of historical consciousness. Insofar as, for Hegel, truth does not coincide with the individual consciousness, this cannot be explained on account of something like Hegel's 'superior intellect'. Rather, Hegel explains this insight into history by the coincidence of himself writing from the perspective of the end of European history. This is the end of its *Geschichte* rather than its *Historie*, which is to say that there will still be lots of historical events, while essentially nothing will be changing. Hegel saw history as beginning in ancient Greece. Insofar as it was a history of alienation, expressed by the contradictions in historical life, moving this world onwards, the end of history comes about by the surmounting of this alienation. According to Hegel, to simplify a little, this happens with the Napoleonic wars, which brought the French revolution to the rest of Europe, and with Hegel's identification of the history of philosophy with the philosophy of history. Hegel thus knows what Napoleon does and Napoleon does what Hegel knows, precisely because both are doing what their historical being demands of them.

But here lies Hegel's danger. While he criticized the Enlightenment for its abstract idea of thought, leading it to a disdain of history, here too the present suddenly turns into the highest moment of mankind. At this 'end of history' it thus becomes evident that there is something exceeding the limitations of history, namely the *Weltvernunft*, the 'world-reason', the logic immanent to all these contradictions having moved the world and proving itself capable of bringing them to a resolution. Hegel's dangers are, then, threefold: (1) the divinization of reason, (2) the undermining of the exemplary nature of the past, and (3) the claim that affirmation of life is possible only from the perspective of its end. Let us look at these briefly.

Hegel's philosophy is a panlogism, arguing that reason proves itself capable of collecting together the whole of existence, of making our life absolutely meaningful. What could be wrong with this? We have seen it before: once one has become everything, there is nowhere to go, which means that life ends up meaningless. Life, as Nietzsche shows again and again, is finite and it thus needs a finite horizon in which it can exist. But this is to say that it can affirm itself only in such limitation. 'Every divinization of abstracted concepts, of state, people, humankind, or the "world process"', on the other hand, 'has the disadvantage that it lightens the load of the individual and hence alleviates its responsibility' (7/662). While this might sound good to our ears, it means that the individual loses her relation to the world as that which she is responsible for.

The second problem concerning the exemplary nature of the past will become clearer once we turn to the three forms of history as Nietzsche outlines them in *On the Advantages and Disadvantages of History for Life*. He asks there how creation is possible in history, considering that we cannot understand it in terms of ideals or utopias. If reason does not stand outside of history, are we then not imprisoned in history and forced to repeat it infinitely? The idea of the new, as Nietzsche argues, is a theological idea, so how can there be anything new in history, once God has died? Nietzsche's answer to this question depends on the exemplary nature of the past. If we can look back at history and see greatness, then that means that greatness is possible in history. This is what Nietzsche will call 'Monumental History', as being inspired by the great 'monuments' of the past. But if, like Hegel, one understands our presence as the highest point of history, then all that is past appears small and insignificant in comparison. While now, at the end of history, the whole of history seems meaningful, it is so only in respect of its movement towards our presence. All 'greatness' of the past is thus relative to our own existence, and if there is nothing great in the past, then greatness seems impossible: 'Every attempt to understand the present as a high point ruins this presence, in that it denies the exemplary significance of history' (7/646).

The third problem concerns the question of an affirmation of life. For both Hegel and Nietzsche the task of philosophy is to make an affirmation of life possible. To look at history from the perspective of life means for Nietzsche to be able to say yes to life, but to do so on its own terms. The affirmation of finite life from the perspective of absolute life, on the other hand, has always put life into perspective and thus still confers the ultimate legitimation to death, as that which Hegel calls the absolute master.

Hegel's affirmation of existence from the perspective of the highest maturity of judgement, which in the evening of existence understands itself as identical with its world, stands thus in opposition to Nietzsche's affirmation of life from the perspective of the childland of creation, for which history is a constant beginning without end. The Hegelian horizon of history is thus closed and only understood in its closure, while the Nietzschean horizon of history is moving within the horizon of the infinite. While for Hegel the end of history promises to recollect everything that has happened in it, Nietzsche's history without an end promises that nothing is lost only insofar as everything will return. To affirm life is thus possible only on account of the despair and the hope of the teaching of the *Eternal Return of the Same*. The ephemeral nature of existence is here valued in 'the search for an eternity of everything: is it allowed to pour the most precious ointments and wines into the sea? – and my consolation is that everything that has been is eternal: – the sea will again wash it ashore' (13/43).

For Nietzsche to say that he stands in opposition to Hegel is thus to say that life has to be affirmed independently of a universal form of reason. Hegel was right in seeing that logic itself is a product of history and that it, therefore, will never come to an end. But this means not only that consciousness is not in possession of its own truth, but also that logic is in essence not at all logical. This is why Nietzsche complains about the Hegelian idea of the dialectic as an unfounded philosophical optimism. To clarify his opposition to Hegel, Nietzsche says: 'I see in logic itself a form of unreason and chance. We attempt to understand the evolution of the human being on account of the greatest unreason, that is, without any reason' (11/253).

iv. OF THE ADVANTAGES AND DISADVANTAGES OF HISTORY FOR LIFE

The real problem of history is then not one of memory but one of forgetting, yet not a forgetting as ignorance, but as the enclosure in a horizon within which life becomes possible. If this horizon is too broad or even disappearing completely, then the alienation of life from its world ensues. If the horizon is too limited, then again, life becomes passive as it lacks the space necessary for its development. Human life is impossible without history and it becomes impossible with the modern attempt to dissolve the whole of history into knowledge, as this means to delimit the horizon of life. To live historically means for the human being to live its finitude in a positive way. It lives on a constant tightrope walk between too much and too little history, without being able consciously to draw the line between the two. Without memory the human being would live like an animal, without past or future, while without forgetting it would be confronted with the truth, namely that there is only becoming, while life cannot exist in pure becoming. 'As a proper pupil of Heraclitus, he [for whom becoming was the absolute truth] would not dare to lift his hand' (HL 62).

Not only is the idea of truth without becoming the figure of death – as Plato has already described it – but in the presence of pure becoming there is that same death once again. The *Will to Truth* is thus quite contradictory. Human life is that life which cannot exist without truth, while truth at the same time threatens life. *Fiat veritas pereat vita*, as Nietzsche argues in the essay on history, which is to say, roughly translated: when truth becomes, then life perishes. One might have equally said that human life is that life which cannot exist except in relation to its past. But this relation to its past is necessarily tragic. While the child lives undisturbed by past or future, one day it will

> understand the phrase 'it was', that password with which struggle, suffering and boredom approach man to remind him what his existence basically is – a never to be completed imperfect tense. And when death finally brings longed-for forgetfulness it also robs him of the present and of existence and impresses its seal on this knowledge: that existence is only an uninterrupted having-been, a thing which lives by denying itself, consuming itself, and contradicting itself. (HL 9)

To speak about the tragic here is to say that the human being has to find an equilibrium between memory and forgetting, without, as we said, being able to make use of rational choice. The healthy attitude to history is not grounded on an absolute memory that recollects the whole of historical becoming, but on an active forgetting, which is literally to say, of activities that allow for a forgetting not as an act of consciousness, but as a practical way to relate to history. In other words, to say that forgetting is the basis of memory is to say that I cannot leave it to reason to say what should be remembered and what forgotten. In this case I would have to remember what to forget. This is why Nietzsche concludes that historical knowledge is not a question of conscious representation but of the various actions that historical existence requires.

If everything that is, is insofar as it is historical, then we can easily distinguish three moments of historical existence. Something has to be brought into existence, it has to be held within existence and, for there to be a future, it has finally to be returned to inexistence. These three modes of creation, preservation and destruction Nietzsche discusses under the forms of Monumental, Antiquarian and Critical History. Life has to find an equilibrium between these three forms, built on an equilibrium found within each of these forms. For example, antiquarian history has the task of preserving what has been created by monumental history. It does so by means of the veneration of the old. But if this veneration becomes overbearing, the human being will invest anything old with value and will not be able to value anything new. Equally with critical history, if it becomes overbearing, just about anything appears as worthy of destruction, thereby leading to the judgement that life itself has no worth.

The greatest miracle of history is thus that the new is possible at all. To create something new within history always implies a certain contradiction, in that this creation is either an effect of a prior cause, in which case it finds its meaning in the past and is thus nothing new at all, or it is something that stands out in history, thereby being a creation precisely in that it breaks the 'causal chain'. It is for this reason that Nietzsche calls this mode of history monumental history. Here creation becomes possible first in that the human being realizes that it was once possible. To see the great work of art arising in the past means that creation has existed and thus can exist. It is thus that the artist takes inspiration not from 'what has been', but from the sheer 'that it has been'; which is to say that it is not understood as a copy of that which has been, but as a copy only of the great moment. The prime example for such monumental history Nietzsche sees in the Renaissance, which he understands as the greatest historical movement since the Greek age. *Renaissance* literally means 'rebirth', and the Renaissance artists took a lot of inspiration from the Greek age. And yet they did not copy it; they did not attempt to become Greek, but created out of the possibility of artistic creation that is classical Greece. In the language we introduced earlier, they were interested in the *Geschichte*, the effective history, not in the *historische* detail.

We can see here the relation between the questions of history and education. A successful education achieves the insertion of the pupil into history. The pupil will first have to learn to bear the weight of history, then to destroy this weight, in order then to become able to act. The stage of the camel thus corresponds to Antiquarian History, that of the lion to Critical History and that of the child, freed for creation, to Monumental History.

To clarify this notion of creation, we may look at the traditional idea of the education of a painter. She would first have been instructed in admiring the great works of art by copying them. The historical 'miracle' of this instruction consists in the fact that while being taught to repeat works of the past, the aim consists in the artist finding her own style of expression, the possibility of repeating the greatness of historical art, by painting something new. Without the great works of the past, they would not even have been able to choose themselves as artists, and in that respect, without history there would not be any art. What is important here, for Nietzsche, is that the notion of creation escapes all attempts at understanding. The understanding understands in that it refers what it tries to understand to its cause, but insofar as a work of art can be called 'great', it does not have a cause. It is, then, possible to teach how to copy great works of art, while it is not directly possible to teach the creation of works of art. The artist, whether we take her in the narrow sense or in the broader sense that Nietzsche has in mind when speaking about the self-creation of humankind, is for this reason always unintelligible to herself as much as to us.

Nietzsche put this a bit more complicatedly in the 'Second Untimely Meditation', where he calls the artist Raphael a *natura naturans*, or a creative nature. *Natura naturans* is a concept that Nietzsche takes from Spinoza, in whose pantheistic system God is described as existing inseparably from the world. For this reason Spinoza can say, in his *Ethics*, that God or Nature are two names for the same thing, so that one only needs to distinguish between *natura naturans*, nature insofar as she is active – literally translated as 'naturing nature' – and *natura naturata*, nature insofar as she is passive – 'natured nature'. These two relate to each other like freedom and necessity, or like art and science, which is to say that 'natured nature' can be understood in a scientific way, so to speak, as if it were dead matter, while 'naturing nature' is on principle unknowable. And yet, creating and understanding here still refer to the same 'thing'. If you compare these points to Nietzsche's claims concerning history, you can see that the scientist is limited to considering the results of the creative process, while the artist, insofar as she has become indistinguishable from the world, draws 'her' creations from nature. Creation is thus possible only by way of a concrete immersion in history.

Modern life finds itself suffering from history. This suffering Nietzsche calls the historical malady. And yet, insofar as it is impossible to transcend history as such, Nietzsche and we ourselves still inhabit this malady. Consequently we can see the contradiction in our occupation with history: insofar as we try to understand the possibility of creation in history, these three moments of creation, preservation and destruction all belong to the problem of creation. Yet insofar as we do have a problem with such creation, we enter into an investigation of the limits and values of history. Such investigation we call a critique. From here, therefore, Nietzsche is developing a critical account of history, so that we are looking at the whole of creation, preservation and destruction from the perspective of the destruction immanent to critique. Today we are, as Kant has said, in the age of critique and everything has to submit to such critique. But critique, while having a valuable part to play in history, makes history unbearable once it becomes overbearing.

It seems that all three forms of history can be seen from the perspective of life as well as from that of critique, and these forms of history appear progressively as those of either life-affirming strength or life-negating weakness. In other words, we can see that antiquarian history, for example, is built more on a sentiment than on account of pure reason and objective judgement. And yet, even critical history, which seems to be the subjugation of anything to the faculty of critique, is a kind of unreason. It destroys blindly since nothing in the world has an absolute legitimation and hence everything appears to it worthy of destruction.

The problem posed throughout the 'Second Untimely Meditation' is the following: Nietzsche distinguishes three forms of history, one of which is called *critical history*. All these forms have 'equal' rights at different moments; all these forms can be employed positively as well as negatively. Yet the historical moment at which critical history comes into its own is precisely that at which the human being entertains a relation to history which can be described as an illness, as *historical malady*. Furthermore, this moment is the very moment at which, motivated by this illness, Nietzsche writes a critique of history. The text we are reading is consequently concerning a critical history in the age characterized by an overbearing mass of critical history; in the end, as Nietzsche says, this essay has itself a very modern style.

v.   FINDING A STYLE TO PHILOSOPHIZE

The question of history is thus posed by Nietzsche in two steps. The first considers the analysis of history as we live it in the age of historicism; the second concerns our ability to act against the historical malady without being able to step outside of it. Life needs a closed historical horizon, while the modern prevalence for critical history does not allow for such closure. This is because this prevalence of critical history leads to the conclusion that our relation to the world as such and to its historical reality is given only through the judgement of the intellect. To criticize this prevalence appears, then, impossible, as it would involve a critique of the understanding by means of the understanding.

And yet we have already seen that the attempt to find an equilibrium within and between the three different forms of history cannot be achieved by the understanding. Neither Monumental History nor Antiquarian History and not even Critical History has a 'rational basis'. They are unable to understand themselves fully and the attempt at such understanding rather exacerbates the problem. The solution can thus not be found on the level of reason, but only on the level of style. For Nietzsche, who wants to address the problem of the historical malady, there thus arises the issue of a style of thinking as the most urgent question. This is the central problem of the essay *On the Advantages and Disadvantages of History for Life*: how can one undertake philosophy with the aim of addressing the problem of nihilism, given that this nihilism is a result of philosophy? In section 10 of the 'Second Untimely Meditation' Nietzsche hence writes that his own work, necessarily, suffers from 'its modern character, a character marked by weakness of personality' (HL 58).

The analysis of history is thus developed by Nietzsche into a critique of modern culture as a lack of style. This weakness of personality refers us back to the modern distinction between mind and body. We have already seen that reducing the question of knowledge to the rationality of the mind does away with any necessity of considering the style of thinking, insofar as it depends on the distinction between form and content. In the end we say that it does not matter how we say something; all that matters is what we say. Yet if thought is not independent from the individuated body, then the question that it raises is the question of the unity of the thinking being. This unity Nietzsche attempts to grasp as what he calls 'the great style'. The answer to philosophical questions will then be given by way of the action of the human being through which its style constitutes itself.

Yet this question of style cannot be reduced to the level of the individual. A historical view of mankind cannot abstract from society, from a society that integrates, but, consequently, that also unifies. The unity that a people needs does not exclude its change, and not even its change through being affected from the outside. Vice versa, as with any other entity, the higher the ability to be affected, the higher the power of a people – as long as in that process it remains a historically existing people. What Nietzsche criticizes is a society in which it makes no difference from which culture you originate, in which it is of no consequence who you are. While such a society might seem at first to be a just society, it turns out to be a society that does not do justice to anyone in particular, precisely insofar as it is an indifferent society; that is, one in which it makes no difference who you are or even *if you are*. To such an indifferent society, which might even express its truth in the words of Margaret Thatcher, namely that 'there is no such thing as society', Nietzsche opposes the following words:

> The culture of a people in contrast to . . . barbarism has once been designated . . . as unity of artistic style in all expressions of life of a people; . . . the people that can be called cultured must in reality be a living unity and not fall apart so miserably into an inside and an outside, a content and a form. (HL 25)

It is because of the limitlessness of the modern historical horizon that the European turns inward. It is because there is nothing alien outside the subject that the subject withdraws into itself; and it has to do so, precisely because of the indifferently identical nature of all subjects. For this reason Nietzsche denounces the differentiation of inside and outside as an effect of modernity. Insofar as all human subjects are declared to be essentially the same, all that is left to them is their own interiority. While these human subjects are, for the very same reason, themselves stale and only empty forms, they pursue only those pleasures which put neither themselves nor the world at stake. The human being of modernity will finally seek nothing other than empty experiences, during which it experiences itself as indifferently anybody, and the world as indifference itself. While we nowadays often proclaim that there has never been an age that has valued human life and human happiness more highly than ours, an indifferent world can only harbour indifferent subjects.

This human individual, who no longer plays any role in society, who is regarded as being the more healthy the more he leads an unobtrusive existence, enjoys nothing more than a knowing which leaves him unharmed. He thirsts for that which does not make any claim on him. The perfect form of this knowing is journalism, the trading of distinct pieces of information, which distinguish themselves from each other neither through their content nor through the way that they affect the knower, but through their news value. Modern life is thus somewhat akin to what Søren Kierkegaard (1813–55) called an 'aesthetic existence', which is to say, an existence reduced to an empty stream of 'stimulating' experiences. Kierkegaard's chief example for such a life is the figure of Don Juan, who runs from experience to experience without these ever having any effect on him. This journalistic culture of modernity

> gives rise to a habit of not taking actual things too seriously any more, this gives rise to the 'weak personality' . . .; in externals one finally becomes ever more casual and indolent and widens the critical gulf between content and form to the point of insensitivity to barbarism, if only the memory is stimulated ever anew, if only ever new things to be known keep streaming in to be neatly put on display in the cases of memory. (HL § 4, p. 25)

This critique of our age seems so absolute that one might wonder how Nietzsche conceives of being able to do anything. This age can only criticize the past and thereby uproots the future. How can one be untimely? We have seen that we have to look at historical science from the perspective of life, but what does this perspective give us? It does not provide us with good arguments; all it gives us, first of all, is a feeling. There is hope, because a feeling has given rise to the critique of history. This feeling is a feeling of youth, of life expressing its stance against its time. First of all it is thus not a question of what arguments Nietzsche has given, but of the motivation of these arguments. This feeling does not lead to a solution of the problem, but it leads to a realization of the problem.

As we have seen a couple of times, the first distance that one can take towards one's age consists in the realization of the illness, and *knowing that one is ill is the first step to healing*. As this healing has to be understood as the move away from illness, it takes the form of a medicine. Now most medicines are indistinguishably poisons. They often do not work against an illness directly, but prepare or help the body to deal with the illness. Nietzsche here, for the first time, formulates the response to nihilism as an active nihilism:

> The origin of historical education – and its inner quite radical contradiction with the spirit of a 'new age', a 'modern consciousness' – this origin *must* itself in turn be historically understood, history *must* itself dissolve the problem of history, knowledge *must* turn its sting against itself – this threefold *must* is the imperative of the spirit of the 'new age' if it really does contain something new, mighty, original and a promise of life. [HL § 8, p. 45]

These three steps – (1) 'the origin of historical education . . . *must* itself . . . be historically understood'; (2) 'history *must* itself dissolve the problem of history'; and (3) 'knowledge *must* turn its sting against itself' – constitute an unfolding of the problem, in that they move from the surface phenomenon to its underlying root cause. Critical history was the idea that knowledge undermines every value in the name of truth. But once knowledge turns its sting against itself, once it asks what truth is good for, it will proceed to wonder, in the name of truth, if it itself is true. This is the formulation for the need of an absolutely sceptical philosophy. And it is absolute in that it does not try to dismantle our beliefs in order to see whether there is something underpinning them which can no longer be doubted.

From here follow the three phases of Nietzsche's work which we have outlined above. First of all there is the 'critical history of critical history', that is of our present, and that is what Nietzsche embarks on in the three great sceptical works, in *Human, All too Human*, in *Dawn*, and in *The Gay Science*. The project followed in these writings, in the work occupying him in all seriousness over the ensuing eight years, had thus already been conceived here in the essay *On the Advantages and Disadvantages of History for Life*. This project takes its strength from the hope that the critical attitude will finally lead to the solution of the problem itself.

But what is there to hope for from such an active nihilism? As Nietzsche himself said, he is one of the three great nihilists of the nineteenth century, but with the hope of getting back to 'some-thing'. We are thus back to the fundamental question of history, namely the question of the self-creation of the human being. This idea of getting back to 'some-thing' then works on account of Monumental History. This was always the answer to an overwhelm-ing feeling that there cannot be anything new in history, that every-thing just follows from the past and can thus be understood as the effect of a cause. Similarly, we think of our nature as something given and immutable. But looking at history we have seen that this is far from the truth; that, indeed, what we take to be the nature of things has been created at some point. And, if that was possible once, it should be possible once again. This is, so to speak, the attempt to supplant our nature by another one. This new, second nature cannot be seen as a development of the first, as the first does not allow for such a development.

> At best we may bring about a conflict between our inherited, innate nature and our knowledge, as well as a battle between a strict new discipline and ancient education and breeding; we implant a new habit, a new instinct, a second nature so that the first nature withers away. It is an attempt, as it were, *a posteriori* to give oneself a past from which one would like to be descended: – always a dangerous attempt because it is so difficult to find a limit in denying the past and because second natures are mostly feebler than the first. (HL 22)

This new and creative manner of understanding history would be strongly adverse to 'what we call historical sense', namely the ability 'increasingly to lose this sense of surprise, no longer to be exces-sively astonished by anything, finally to tolerate everything' (HL 41). Against 'the analytic and inartistic trend of our time' (HL 39), the historian, as an artist, 'must have the strength to recast the well known into something never heard before' (HL 37). The genuine historian has, then, to counter the feeling of indifference that gov-erns modernity. The engagement with history will free the human being from the feeling of being determined by a past in order to open it up towards its fate – which is to say, towards its future. It therefore has to liberate it from its presence. The best summary of Nietzsche's thought concerning history can thus be found in his essay on 'Schopenhauer as Educator', where he formulates the task of the philosopher, as the genuine historian, as making the present imperceptible.

> Everything present is intrusive, it affects and determines the eye even against the wishes of the philosopher; and, involuntarily, it gains too much weight in the final account. For this reason the philosopher has to appraise the difference of his time against others and, in that he for himself overcomes the present, he also has to overcome the present in the image that he paints of life. He has to make the present imperceptible, he has to, so to speak, paint it over. (1/361)

CHAPTER 3

OF SCIENCE AND NIHILISM

New conflicts. – Following Buddha's death, his shadow was still exhibited for centuries in a cave. . . . God is dead; but thinking of the way of human beings, there may still be caves for thousands of years in which his shadow will be shown. – And we – we have to overcome his shadow, too.

The best-known phrase from Nietzsche's works is the affirmation that 'God is dead'. We too easily tend to think that this might still have been a radical statement in the nineteenth century, while today it has become a perfectly accepted opinion. Some people are atheists, some are not, but being an atheist is no longer anything shocking.

We are, then, dealing with the question of the existence of God mostly as with any other question, namely as one of belief. Some people believe in God, some do not, and everyone should be free to make up their own mind with respect to their beliefs. We have encountered Nietzsche's critique of 'beliefs' a few times already and here again we will see that the problem for us is that beliefs are generally indifferent to each other as much as to the world. That is to say, we easily think that one can believe in God or not, without this having much of an effect on the other beliefs we might hold. Therefore we do not think that with the death of God we have lost much, besides one item of belief amongst others. Nietzsche, on the other hand, tries to persuade us that with the death of God everything changes and nothing will remain the same. The *Death of God* is then the name for this transitional phase which he, above, called nihilism.

i. NIHILISM: GOD IS DEAD

This is the situation that Nietzsche describes in section 125 of *The Gay Science*. Here 'the madman' runs to the marketplace and announces to the people standing around there that he seeks God. The people make fun of him; laughingly they ask whether God has got lost, gone into hiding or might have emigrated. Nietzsche introduces the people on the market square as 'many of those who did not believe in God'. Strangely, the words 'many' and 'those' are capitalized in the original, indicating that these non-believers stand in for the many that make up our present-day societies.

These are 'many' already because they have, without realizing it, lost that which kept them together, namely religion. And they are many insofar as they think about themselves having beliefs that they hold 'personally'. They might thus share beliefs with others or disagree about these, but such sharing is not much different from various objects sharing attributes. As little as a red table is affected by belonging to the group of all red tables, so is the one who believes in such a way affected by belonging to the group of all believers. In other words, without the communion of religion, human beings lose the essential bond between them, thus becoming isolated units. We have seen this in the last chapter when speaking about modern individuals withdrawing into their private, individual lives, because of the opposition between inside and outside, and we have already called this nihilism. If the beliefs I hold or do not hold are indifferent to myself and to the world as such, then I can neither believe in the value of my knowledge, nor believe in the value of the 'outside' world. The notion of thought as indifferent belief is itself nihilistic, which is to say that it does not matter whether I then believe or do not believe in this nihilism. Equally, it seems, those who do 'believe' in God are atheists as much as those who do not. God is dead and whatever we might believe or not believe does not make a big difference.

The many thus do not believe in God, but they do not seem to suffer from this either. On the contrary, they are laughing. Nihilism, as Nietzsche has said, affects us all the more as we remain unaware of it. Nietzsche does not then attempt to persuade people who believe in God that they should not do so. He does not provide arguments for or against the existence of God. Rather he tries to convince us atheists that the world does not remain the same now that God has died. And yet, this is precisely what we tend to think, namely that the world itself is today the same as always, except that we no longer believe in God.

But how can one say that God has died? Does not God either exist or not exist? And, if he had once existed, should he, as immortal, not always exist and do so by necessity? And if the death of God implies that he has once existed, what precisely is it that we have lost with his death? Indeed, one of the most influential arguments for the existence of God, the ontological argument, first conceived of by St Anselm (1033–1109), proves that God cannot not exist, which is to say that the existence of God is logically necessary. While we can imagine a world without this or that animal, maybe even without rivers, mountains or beautiful islands, we cannot think of a world without God. But, without going into the details of this argument, must it not necessarily be wrong, considering that we are well capable of thinking of a world without God? In the end, Plato had already given proofs for the existence of God, and the need for a proof seems to imply that there are people who do not believe.

But we only need to look a bit more closely at these arguments to see that their stress lies on the notion of 'world' rather than a belief in a divine entity. Plato provides his argument as an alternative for the punishment of atheists. Why should atheists be punished? Because they commit the highest crime against the community. The human being is the halfway house between heaven and earth, which is to say, the world is that which is opened between heaven and earth. But without divine existence there is no 'between'. In other words, everything that characterizes humanness as such – thinking, freedom and hence political self-determination – is possible only with respect to divine existence. The atheist, Plato thus argues, takes away the freedom and humanness of all, which leads to the conclusion that atheism is a crime worse than murder. Today we might say, following Descartes' distinction between the thinking mind and the extended 'world', that if the 'world' itself was one of merely mechanical relations between material things, then human life as such would become impossible.

Nearly 1,500 years after Plato, St Anselm's argument makes this point a bit clearer. We might have been thinking that an argument for the existence of God is designed to persuade those who do not believe. Thus one of the rebukes made to St Anselm was that his argument would not sway anyone who does not believe. Strangely enough, St Anselm responds to this criticism that he is not speaking to the idiot, who has said in his heart that God does not exist. Has he just run out of arguments, moving to insults? Or is there a better reason for this? There are two points of interest to us. First, St Anselm is quite happy with the fact that a good argument will never persuade anyone of the existence of God. Indeed, one might think that the mere idea of proving God's existence is, next to being impossible, even heretic. As Anselm makes clear in his original, ontological argument, God exists in faith and if he does not exist in faith, no argument will change anything about this: if the heart says no, it matters not what the mind is pondering.

As a consequence it is only those who have faith in God who can understand the argument, while, as Anselm said, he cannot persuade the idiot. But why would somebody who has faith need an argument? It cannot be to prop up an otherwise faltering faith, as we have just shown that it is the faith which has to underlie the proof. And why is the atheist an idiot? An idiot is someone who, though maybe very intelligent, never manages to touch on reality by means of his words. That is, his words do not attach themselves to reality, but to some other world, existing only in his mind. Thus when Nietzsche, in the *Antichrist*, calls Jesus Christ an idiot, this is not meant as a simple insult, but is saying that when Jesus seems to be speaking about this world, he really always talks about another world. When he speaks about life, for example, he really speaks about eternal life – which is to say, about death. Jesus Christ, as Nietzsche says, speaks only in metaphors and thus never speaks the truth.

St Anselm's argument, therefore, tries to locate the reason for which somebody whose 'heart' has faith in God can be assured of not remaining an idiot, which is to say that his faith will bring together his thought and reality. Believing in God thus makes possible the human world as a world in which I live and about which I can communicate with others within my religious community. And this is why I cannot think about a world without God. Without God I thus think about nothing at all, as thought would have lost its relation to a world.

This is not an isolated argument by an eleventh-century priest. We could find the same conviction in René Descartes' work *Meditations on First Philosophy*, which we have already heard about a few times.

Descartes presents us with six meditations, which begin with the possibility that all knowledge in the proper sense of the word might be impossible, and end with the idea of a world established on the notion of a certainty of truth. Let us just briefly look for a reason why Meditations Three and Five are dedicated to two different arguments for the existence of God. At the beginning of the second meditation we find the famous conclusion that however much I might be wrong and deluded in any or all of my thoughts, I cannot doubt that I am thinking. Therefore I cannot doubt the images about which I am thinking either. For example, I have experiences while hiking through the countryside. I see, perhaps, bunny rabbits and rivers. While I might be logically able to doubt that these really do exist, I cannot doubt that I see them, in the same way as I might, after waking up, doubt that the monster I dreamt about has any real existence in the world, while not being able to doubt that I dreamt of this monster.

The reality of my experience is thus given indubitably once I am given – so why do we need these proofs for the existence of God? Literally, as Meditation Three makes clear, in order to be able to speak about something which exists outside of my mind. The first proof thus establishes that at least one idea in my mind, namely that of God, points to his existence outside of my mind. But why do we need another proof in Meditation Five, which is a variant of Anselm's ontological argument? Was the first proof not good enough? No, the second proof is there in order to show that that entity which does exist outside of my mind is a God who guarantees that all my clear and distinct ideas relate to a reality outside of my mind and that this reality is the same for all other human beings. It thus instigates my community with a world and with others. Without God I would thus be condemned to live the life of an idiot, of someone who speaks only about a 'world' inside his head.

Now we know why the person who seeks God in section 125 of *The Gay Science* is a madman and why those that he addresses are the 'many', and we can equally see why the annunciation of the death of God takes such a dramatic form in saying that nothing will remain the same following this death of God:

What were we doing when we unchained this earth from its sun? Whither is it moving now? Whither are we moving? Away from all suns? Are we not plunging continually? Backward, sideward, forward, in all directions? Is there still any up or down? Are we not straying as through an infinite nothing? (GS 181)

The notion of the human world, which gives us a space in which to live, an above and a below, a direction for life itself, a truth that grants us sanctuary – all that is gone with the death of God. All that is left is an 'infinite nothing', without measure or valuation, without good or evil.

But of what value is this insight into the reality of the death of God? Are not the 'many' happy and laughing, while the madman seems to suffer? And is the madman trying to warn us, so that we may quickly return to the sanctuary of faith? Is he not saying that '*we have killed* [God] – you and I. All of us are his murderers' (GS 181)? And may we not be able to undo this deed? We have seen that God exists in faith and that this faith is something given in the 'heart'. But this 'heart' is not swayed by the intellect, thus not by good argument, and not by the insight into our need for him. To have killed God is an act that is final and that cannot be reversed. 'God is dead. God remains dead. And we have killed him' (GS 181).

With the death of God we have lost everything: all we have left is nothing; that is, nihilism. It is not only that monarchies have lost their legitimation, that war can no longer be fought 'in the name of God', that individual nations have lost their claim to be chosen by God, that the human being is no longer the one who finds its legitimation in being created in the image of God, that there is no longer a religious *fatum* which would allow me to act without thinking – but the human being itself, the idea of a communal world, of a truth that allows us to exist together, the idea of a separation of body and mind, all these have vanished.

We saw that Kant was able to understand the world of knowing without reference to God, but as soon as he thought about human freedom, about morality, this showed itself impossible without the imperative voice of God. We might still think of good and bad in the sense of utility, but these are no longer the moral categories of Good and Evil with their binding character. Thus we might say 'thou shalt not steal', because what would happen to our lives if everyone stole?, but that is a calculative proposition, which I can address by all kinds of means, even by saying that not everyone will steal, as most are too timid, and finally by calculating the risk of detection against possible gain. To think after the death of God is thus to think *beyond Good and Evil.*

The idiot was the one whose words failed to attach themselves to a world, the one in whose experience language consisted merely of empty words. Indeed, without God and without the idea that all languages go back to their origin in the divine word, even the idea of communication has become difficult. Nietzsche had addressed this problem in the early essay 'On Truth and Lying in a Non-Moral Sense'. Here he begins with the argument that the idea of truth is not the original function of the intellect, which first must have been used as an instrument of deception. Where the tiger has sharp teeth, the human being has its intellect. In other words, at the beginning of language stands the lie. It is only on account of the formation of societies, both demanding the limitation of lying amongst its members and the possibility of an agreement between them, that the idea of truth arises and the obligation to tell the truth. We might as well say that the question of truth is originally a religious question. Following the death of God, which is to say, the end of the idea that language has been given to us in order to speak the truth, Nietzsche argues that

> the genesis of language does not proceed logically in any case, and all the material within and with which the man of truth, the scientist, and the philosopher later work and build, if not derived from never-never-land, is at least not derived from the essence of things. (TL 83)

Truth is thus always a human truth. It does not speak the truth of the world as such, but 'only' of the objective world, that is, the human world insofar as these objects are objects for subjects. What then is truth, Nietzsche asks, and concludes:

> a movable host of metaphors, metonymies, and anthropomorphisms: in short, a sum of human relations which have been poetically and rhetorically intensified, transferred, and embellished, and which, after long usage, seem to a people to be fixed, canonical, and binding. Truths are illusions which we have forgotten are illusions; . . . (TL 84)

But the community within which these metaphors speak is itself lost with the death of God. Consequently I am reduced to speaking about my private 'world', my idiosyncratic beliefs; I speak as an idiot in metaphors.

But why should we be left with nothing at all? Do we not exist in the age of the natural sciences, which have achieved an unparalleled understanding of the world? Is not the death of God the birth of the Modern Sciences? It might be true that the idea of the human being as a halfway house between heaven and earth has come to an end and that the 'biological determinist' has inherited the truth from the divine soul, but do we not know much more than we have ever known? And do we not agree on such knowledge as an 'object-ive' knowledge, precisely by making it independent of any particu-lar subject and its experiences? Today, is somebody like Richard Dawkins not in the right when he turns the tables on Anselm, pro-claiming loudly that it is the believer who is an idiot, while we atheists are much more clever, much more rational and in possession of many more truths?

But such an idea depends on the view that the modern natural sciences are conceived in opposition to Christian theology, that they constitute a break with the truth of Christianity, while Nietzsche argues that there is nothing new in the 'scientific world view'. As we will see, the age of science cannot be understood as a new age, containing 'something new, mighty, original and a promise of life' (HL 45), but is the phenomenon of the demise of Christianity itself. It is the same will to truth that operates in modern science; it is the nihilistic phenomenon of knowledge turning its sting against itself, positing the question of whether this will to truth is itself in truth. Insofar as the 'scientific world view' reduces the world to a sum total of facts, it does not leave any space for such a will, which is to say that it does not leave a space for life itself. But as Nietzsche argued in the last chapter, every value, including the value of know-ing, has to be seen from the perspective of life, so that the modern sciences appear themselves as nihilistic.

What is overlooked all too easily today is that the question of the death of God is for Nietzsche not one that can be reduced to ques-tions of morality, of freedom, or to the notion of a supersensible existence granting meaning to the sensible world. Rather, insofar as the death of God concerns us, who live in the age of science, it is itself the question of the value and truth of modern science. This is what the 'many' on the market square fail to realize: that the death of God concerns the untenability of our 'world view'; and that is to say, of science. This critique of science pervades Nietzsche's whole work and it is not too surprising, thinking of the relation between Christianity and science, that the *Antichrist* will deal not only with a denunciation of Christian theology but also with a critique of the idea of truth in the modern sciences. True atheism has to bring about the death of God in its concrete sense, and this is why 'atheism', understood as a mere question of belief, hides its real significance as the question of the truth of science.

We have seen before, in the cases of idealism and realism, that when considered on the level of abstract ideas these appear as opposites, while considered from the level of history they appear as two interdependent phenomena. Here we will see that, again, on the level of abstract ideas we might be thinking that science arises from its contradiction to Christianity, whereas seen in concretion, science appears as the shadow of the dead God, as the leftovers of Christianity after the death of God. Until we realize that the question of the death of God erodes the foundations of our scientific world, we have not understood it at all. Nietzsche will thus deal with science under the title of the 'shadows of God', which we will have to vanquish too. As the madman of section 125 of *The Gay Science* concludes after addressing the 'many' on the market square, 'I have come too early . . . this tremendous event is still on its way, . . . it has not yet reached the ears of men' (GS 182).

ii. FROM THE BIRTH OF TRAGEDY TO THE QUESTION OF SCIENCE

Strangely enough, in the majority of reflections on Nietzsche's thought the question of science does not figure as a central problem. Nietzsche is thought to deal with questions of aesthetics, morality and metaphysics. Thus one thinks of the *Birth of Tragedy*, for example, as a romantic treatment of the classical Greek age from the perspective of a philologist, and of the later works mainly as an elaboration of his critique of Christian morality. And even where readers pick up the notion of science as explicitly posed by Nietzsche, they either point out that the German *Wissenschaft* has a much broader sense than our word 'science', in that it includes the human sciences and even the idea of philosophy as a science, or they allege that, in his middle period, Nietzsche embraced the idea of the modern sciences from the position of a naïve philologist, who had not much of an idea of what science actually is. In the first case it is said that his critique only extends to the science called philology; in the second that there is not much substance to his critique. And yet, what the German *Wissenschaft* retains is that in all these various sciences, from the 'hard' sciences like physics to the 'soft' human sciences, we speak about one problem, namely that with all due attention to the war between the natural and the human sciences, such a war was possible precisely because what are at stake are the methods of all sciences, as the methods on which we base our interpretation of the world and of ourselves.

One 'proof' that is often used for this rebuke against Nietzsche's thought is the 'unscientific' nature of the idea of the *Eternal Return of the Same*, which we are to consider in the next chapter. According to this point the *Eternal Recurrence* is supposed to be a scientific theory, and commentators have picked on a remark made by Nietzsche in the early 1880s, namely that he planned to go to Paris to study science. This wish they interpret as the search for a scientific confirmation of the theory itself. And yet one does not have to think about the idea of *Eternal Recurrence* for a long while to realize that there cannot in principle be any scientific proof or confirmation of it. From here one concludes that Nietzsche was scientifically naïve. Given that we live in the age of science and that any reflection on human life would need to think about the fundamentals of our world, this argument appears as a general invalidation of his thinking. According to this interpretation, the *Zarathustra* then confirms Nietzsche's flight from a misunderstood critique of science into the more beautiful and harmless realm of literature.

In what follows I will show that these claims are quite meaningless, first of all, because Nietzsche thought of science as the main problem of his thinking; and second, because it is completely meaningless to say that philosophical thinking should be based on scientific results. Philosophy is the reflection on the essence of our being and our understanding, or it is nothing. To attempt to turn philosophy into a science, as Nietzsche says, means to 'throw in the towel' (7/710), which is to say, to give up on the idea of a philosophical self-determination of the human being in the face of the deterministic world of science.

For Nietzsche, despite all the criticism of the sciences that we will encounter, this is not a question of making a decision 'for or against' science, as little as the question of the death of God gave rise to a decision 'for or against' belief in God. Such a decision is for Nietzsche quite meaningless, a decision between unquestioned allegiance and ignorance. In other words, the problem of science is for us today unavoidable, and any philosophical thinking that does avoid it is for that reason from the outset a failed thinking. The question of science is thus given not as affirming or negating it, but as the inescapable horizon of contemporary thought: 'Therefore: long live physics! And even more so that which *compels* us to turn to physics – our honesty' (GS 266).

In a new preface to *The Birth of Tragedy*, written 14 years after the book's first publication, Nietzsche makes these remarks about its intent:

What I had got hold of at that time was something fearsome and dangerous, a problem with horns, not necessarily a bull, but at any rate a *new* problem; today I would say that it was the *problem of science* itself, science grasped for the first time as something problematic and questionable. (BT 4f)

But, reading *The Birth of Tragedy*, this does not seem immediately obvious. What he does write about here is the idea of art in classical Greek tragedy, its location between the pictorial arts and music, and therefore, mainly, the idea of two essential drives to art, presented in the form of two Greek deities, namely Apollo as the god of the pictorial arts and Dionysos as the god of music. Apollo is interpreted by Nietzsche as the god of the principle of individuation, and thus as reasonable, as guarding differences and the limits between myself and that which is other, while Dionysos is the god of wine, that is of intoxication, of music and dance as those acts in which one loses one's identity. You can already see that these gods relate to each other like our ideas of being and becoming. Yet, in opposition to our ideas, the relation between being and becoming is here not thought of as something theoretical or conceptual, as something that merely *is*, but as artistic creation.

The classical Greek age comes into existence once these two divinities come together, once Apollo speaks with the voice of Dionysos and Dionysos with the voice of Apollo. Divorced from each other, these fundamental forces do not give rise to artistic greatness. While Apollo represents a knowledge without truth,

Dionysos presents the idea of a truth without knowledge. Indeed, the Dionysian festivities – Dionysos being a rather late arrival among the Greek gods – were originally quite violent and related to human sacrifice. The classical age of the Greeks, the cradle of European culture, has thus arisen from the transformation of religious deities into the force of art. And this age is called the age of art because, as Nietzsche argues, the Greeks saw life itself as art. We have seen this already in our discussion of Hegel in the last chapter. If we want to know a truth about Greece, then we have to look not at scientific investigations or at sociological data. This would be to look from the perspective of our age of science onto the world of the Greeks. Rather we have to try to look at it with their eyes, so far as that is possible, and this means through art itself. This is why Hegel and Nietzsche both reflect on tragedy in order to grasp the truth of Greece.

But what has all this to do with the question of science, which does not seem to find much mention in the book? Europe, as Hölderlin has said, is the movement from 'the fires from the heavens' to 'the clarity of representation', which is to say, the historical movement from the Greek age of art to our age of science. What Nietzsche is thus interested in is this birth of science as the birth of philosophy issuing from the end of the age of art. To understand this historical reality of the sciences thus means that 'the problem of science cannot be recognized within the territory of science' (BT 5). Science is then nothing new and it is not self-founding. Let us take one example to clarify this point. 'Biology' is a Greek word, made up of *bios* and *logos*. Nowadays we translate this as 'the science of life'. But what if life has a problem with this science? Can biology even raise the question 'What is life?', let alone 'What is the meaning of life?' Indeed, it cannot do so. It can look at specific questions within its object domain and it can do so on account of methods which it equally cannot validate. Furthermore, as Nietzsche has pointed out, insofar as it considers facts only, that is, things interpreted as being present, what it calls life would be better called death. We have already encountered this problem in our discussion of Leibniz, who demonstrated that science is restricted to the realm of passive representation, thereby misrecognizing the phenomenon of life.

But the age of science still concerns the creation of a certain form of life. Consequently, and as Nietzsche said above, science is art that has forgotten that it is art, and it is for this reason that we have to look at science from the perspective of art and at art from the perspective of life. To look at science from the perspective of life means to see it as an expression of the will; that is to say, its striving. We have seen in Nietzsche's early essays that he attempts to understand the origin of the sciences from the will to truth. This will to truth is the foundation of the striving for knowledge. As Nietzsche says in section 344 of *The Gay Science*, there is no such thing as a presuppositionless science. 'The question whether truth is needed must not only have been affirmed in advance, but affirmed to such a degree that the principle, the faith, the conviction finds expression: "*Nothing* is needed *more* than truth, and in relation to it everything else has only second-rate value" ' (GS 281). It is this will to truth that Nietzsche attempts, in *The Birth of Tragedy*, to discover in its origin from art. This affirmation today bears such force that in the pathos of science one 'might actually be part and parcel of the decision to prefer a handful of "certainties" to a whole wagonload of beautiful possibilities', as Nietzsche says later in *Beyond Good and Evil* (BGE 5/23). It is this nihilism that expresses itself in the modern age of science. But this will to truth is not only originally moral, it is also a consequence of Christian theology. And it is here that we find the reason for which Nietzsche understands modern science as a shadow of the Christian God. And insofar as Christianity, according to Nietzsche, is 'Platonism for the people', while Plato is the pupil of Socrates, Nietzsche identifies the historical root of science with the Socratic type of thinking, which, in turn, he sees as bringing about the death of the tragic age of the Greeks.

iii. THE BIRTH OF PHYSICS

We began this chapter with the famous quotation from section 108 of the *Gay Science*, according to which 'God is dead', while we still have to 'vanquish his shadows too'. In order to see what Nietzsche means by these shadows, it is sufficient to read on, as section 109 provides a list of these in the form of six warnings. These warnings concern interpretations of the world which derive from the Christian will to truth and they are all related to our interpretation of the world, which we generally think of as physics:

> Let us beware of thinking that the world is a living being . . . Let us even beware of believing that the world is a machine . . . Let

us beware of attributing to it heartlessness or unreason or their
opposites . . . Let us beware of saying that there are laws in
nature . . . Let us beware of saying that death is opposed to life
. . . Let us beware of thinking that the world eternally creates
new things . . . (GS 167f)

However one thinks of the modern natural sciences, without interpreting the world either as an organic existence or a mechanism,
without saying that there are laws in nature, these seem to be impossible. The critique of science thus belongs to the 'de-deification of
nature', as Nietzsche calls this in the same section. The critique
of science is thus part and parcel of the critique of Christianity.

What then is the origin of the modern natural sciences? One
might say that their possibility has been given by Plato, that they
have been conceived in Descartes' thought, that they have been
born in Leibniz's and Newton's work, and that they have been chris-
tened in Kant's critical system. Let us briefly look at these moments
in order to see what Nietzsche is getting at.

The possibility of the natural sciences as objective knowing
depends on the ability to make a distinction between the true world
of ideas and the world of appearances, as it is given in Plato's philosophy. Here the difference between being and becoming is no
longer understood as the result of artistic praxis, but it is reified.
This is to say that this difference just *is* the case. It is now possible to
look at the world and to describe it by eternally self-same ideas. In
other words, what is given here is a strict distinction between thought
and reality, between the form of explanation and that which is
explained. While for the Greeks there cannot be laws of nature –
because the idea of law is that of commanding and obeying, which
is to say that law belongs to the human community, while nature
does not obey human laws – at least on account of this difference it
will become possible to conceive of such laws in the mathematical
sense. Nietzsche constantly goes back to these points, namely that,
on the one hand, there is something odd in speaking about laws of
nature, while, on the other, there is something even odder about
finding number in nature. Number belongs to logic, which is to say,
to human thought, while the idea of a mathematical science would
then presuppose that nature obeys human thought. In order for
there to be natural law, the law has to exist independently from that
which it rules over. In other words, the law should be independent

from who I am or what I have done. And for the law to be independent, we need a distinction between at least two worlds. While this sounds a bit strange, we will see that this is the conclusion that Kant will give to the problem of science more than 2,000 years later.

The conception of science can be found in Descartes' *Meditations*. Before Descartes, one had thought of the reasons for which a thing is what it is in terms of the 'four causes' of Aristotle. These are the *causas efficiens, formalis, materialis* and *finalis*. In short, in order to explain any particular thing in terms of what it is, I have to account for the form it takes (*formalis*), for the matter it is made out of (*materialis*), for the way that it has come into existence (*efficiens*) and the purpose for which it has been created (*finalis*). As one thought of the world as having been created by God, one could thus think of it in analogy to human production. If I want to explain a knife, I have to explain its production, I have to take a relatively hard material, to which I have to give a form so that it is fit for cutting, and I have to want to cut something. The *causa finalis* is thus that cause which motivates the whole process. But here occurs the problem. As God has created the world, so long as his intentions are something that I on principle cannot understand, I will never be able to understand the world either. The trick by means of which Descartes solves this problem in the Sixth Meditation is first of all quite inconspicuous. He argues that it is quite true that God must have created the world for a purpose, but he has also created me and my ability to represent and understand the world. And yet, he has created me in such a way that these purposes do not appear in my representation. When I look at a tree or at a spider, I cannot see why God has created them. There is, then, a divine legitimation in dealing with the world *as if* there were no final causes, that is, *as if* the world was a mechanism, bereft of souls, which is to say, without beings that move themselves, without freedom.

This idealism, which is able to affirm that truth exists merely in the mind, can completely distinguish the level of thinking from that which this thought explains. Science is thus conceived of as the ability to describe things objectively and to restrict its descriptions to 'clear and distinct' ideas. That is, without final causation the world is no longer to be understood as motivated and all motion can be restricted to dislocation in space. As such I can understand motion by means of restricting movement to the present, i.e. to fact.

As a consequence of this restriction of nature in Descartes we have come to understand the word 'causation' in the exclusive sense of *efficient causation*. Herewith we also find the origin of the difference between natural and human sciences and the reason why we can call the former 'hard' sciences, as the notion of clear and distinct ideas only holds properly for things of nature.

What is important for Nietzsche here is that we find at the beginning of science a separation from questions of theology, while the possibility of this separation is due to theology. The true foundation of science is thus hidden from it. Platonic philosophy and Christian theology, as Nietzsche has argued above, are essentially ahistorical. Consequently, the natural sciences can equally distinguish their truth from their history, thereby convincing themselves that scientific method is independent from its tradition. Historians of science might be interested in and reflect on the way that science has arisen from Christian theology, but the scientist can disregard such historical reflection as inessential to the methods of science. That is to say, the scientist works on account of the conviction that she looks at the world just as it is given in present experience, and it is on this account that we speak of the experiential nature of science. But this experiential essence of the modern sciences does not contradict their mathematical essence; rather, the sciences can be experiential precisely because they are mathematical.

While the task of philosophy is to be untimely, so to speak, to paint over the significance of the present, science is a phenomenon of the will to truth as restricting itself to the present. This is why Nietzsche calls this a reactive will, as it forsakes the significance of its own action, as it no longer believes that it has any part in the world. Not having a part in the world is the necessary condition for having certain knowledge of it, while having achieved this we suddenly hit on the problem of error. This problem had occurred in Descartes: his meditations begin with the notion of a radical doubt, which is to say with the possibility that all that we believe might be wrong. But only three meditations later the question is turned on its head. If the world consists only of clear and distinct ideas, how could there ever have been any error? Should the world not be self-evident? Descartes' answer involves the mismatch between an infinite will and a finite understanding. We make mistakes in our understanding of nature, as we want to understand everything, even that which is not available to the understanding. The only obstacle between my understanding and the world that it understands is thus the delusion of my will.

But let us clarify the point Nietzsche is making here. Science not only competes the reduction of its object to present fact, but equally the reduction of the subject of knowing to the present. When Nietzsche says that the problem of science cannot be understood from within science, this is also because it makes its own problem invisible. It was for the same reasons that the 'many' on the market square were laughing. From here follows the reduction to the present of the knower, in the sense of the inability to understand that the world could be otherwise. This whole figure of thought is rather reminiscent of the problems of Christian revelation. If God is the truth, how could there have been centuries in which there were no Christians? In the end, again, the human being, instead of turning to the question of truth, is much more perplexed by the question 'How could there ever have been error?' In the same vein there are today 'scientists' who decry the 'God delusion', saying that the reason why the truth only appears now is this strange mass-delusion which managed to keep a hold over humans for thousands of years. So we might wonder how people in the twelfth century could be so convinced of the truth of their world, while we forget to ask exactly why it seems so wrong to us. In other words, while complaining about ages that had to be awoken from slumber, we hardly ever wonder if we have good reasons to be so sure about our wakefulness. Here there is, according to Nietzsche, not much of a difference between the thirteenth- and the twenty-first-century inhabitant, insofar as the conviction of righteousness derives from our drives and sensations, which themselves are inherited from nothing but the errors of our history. The more that we thus oppose the tradition of thought, the more we are subjected to it.

We have already seen the significance of Leibniz and Newton with respect to the development of the modern sciences in the first chapter. With the introduction of the notion of force and the principle of the preservation of energy, the distinction between the material truth of the outside world and the formal truth of the mind – that is, the distinction between a world which harbours final causes and its representation as bereft of such causes – has been broken down. The notion of force, as we have seen, represents things in their immediate relation to other things and, which is the main point, it is the idea of reality as completely determinable by number. Now the idea of nature has properly become the object of a mathematical science, without there being anything hidden behind this world. Insofar as Nietzsche's doctrine of the *Eternal Return of the Same* begins with this formulation of science, we need not look at this in more detail here.

There is only one milestone in the history of science to add here in order to understand Nietzsche's critique of science as absolute anthropomorphism of experience. In Descartes we met the problem of knowing that the world is otherwise than we experience it, while being able to ignore this difference. One has always wondered which of the attributes of a thing exist only relative to one's experience and which are attributes of 'the thing itself'. Colour, for example, exists only insofar as I see it. A red object, for example, is one that 'likes' all the colours of the spectrum except red, which it throws back at me. If there is no light, it is not that I cannot see the colour, but the colour does not exist. Descartes argued that it is first of all temporal duration and spatial extension that, conversely, belong essentially to the thing itself. One has thus made a distinction between primary and secondary qualities, a distinction which harbours the difficulty we have just outlined, namely that the objectivity of knowledge suffers from not knowing what we are talking about, the object of experience or the thing as independent from experience. From here followed also the confrontation between idealism and materialism, taking the side of the object and the thing in itself respectively.

While one might think that the sciences would be interested to know the attributes pertaining to the thing in itself, to the thing as absolutely independent from experience, it is difficult to see how this should be possible, considering that we are talking about experiential sciences. Rather, the ideal of the sciences is that of an absolutely objective knowing, which means a knowing that is shared, that is the same for everyone, instead of, so to speak, a knowing of that which is for 'no one'. This reduction of the world to pure objectivity is accomplished in the critical system of Immanuel Kant. Kant demonstrates in the *Critique of Pure Reason* that there are no primary qualities whatever, indeed, that we cannot even make use of the term 'thing-in-itself' in any meaningful sense. What Kant thus has to argue is that even spatial extension and temporal duration depend on our experience. Space and time he thus calls intuitions of human subjectivity. This is to say that, while I myself experience the spatio-temporal world as real, finally it exists as such only for the experience of human beings. Kant calls this his Copernican turn in philosophy. Copernicus was the astronomer who proved that it is not the case that all planets turn around the earth, but that the earth is one of the planets turning around the sun. Kant proved that we do not have to run after things in order to understand them, but that conversely these things adapt themselves to our ways of experience.

With the Kantian formulation of the natural sciences it is finally possible to speak of strict, mathematical laws of nature, and this is precisely insofar as the world now appears completely anthropomorphic, which is to say, in the form of human understanding. While it sounded a bit strange to speak earlier of natural law in the sense of a commanding on the part of the human being and an obeying on the part of nature, this is exactly what can now be proven. As Kant said: 'The understanding does (a priori) not take its laws out of nature, but prescribes these laws to nature' (*Prolegomena*, § 36, p. 79). What Kant can thus demonstrate is the absolute objectivity of scientific knowledge, founded on the universal necessity of human experience. And yet, ultimately, such sciences do not describe or explain nature, but only the necessities of our own existence, which is why Nietzsche says that here we have learned to describe ourselves better:

All that we actually know about the laws of nature is what we ourselves bring to them – time and space, and therefore relationships of succession and number. . . . everything marvellous about the laws of nature, everything that quite astonishes us therein and seems to demand our explanation . . .: all this is completely and solely contained within the mathematical strictness and inviolability of our representations of time and space. But we produce these representations in and from ourselves with the same necessity with which the spider spins. If we are forced to comprehend all things only under these forms, then it ceases to be amazing that in all things we actually comprehend nothing but these forms. For they must all bear within themselves the laws of number, and it is precisely number which is most astonishing in things. All the conformity to law, which impresses us so much in the movement of the stars and in chemical processes, coincides at bottom with those properties which we bring to things. Thus it is we who impress ourselves in this way. (TL 87)

It is on account of this idea of science that Nietzsche calls Kant the 'universal spider', the one who catches all things within the universal net of experience. But this is to say that the sciences give us knowledge of the world in the form of that which is necessarily human. In these sciences we learn nothing about reality except the conditions of our own existence. Nietzsche comes back to this point again and again. When, in *The Gay Science*, he writes a section called 'Long live physics!', he soon turns to question what we would judge to belong to morality rather than to physics, while his legitimation for this is that the sciences are a Christian, that is, a moral phenomenon. As the main question of morality is not that of the rightness of individual action, but the form of human community, Nietzsche can thus look at the sciences as a process of breeding, integrating human beings into society by means of the homogenization of experience.

> Fundamentally the sciences aim at the ascertainment of how the human being – not the individual – perceives the relation to all things and to itself,. . . . That is, a phantom is constructed, and everyone constantly works towards finding that on which everyone has to agree, because it belongs to the essence of the human being. Hereby one has learned that many things which we thought necessary are not so, and that by means of this ascertainment of necessity we have not proved anything concerning reality, besides that the existence of the human being has up to now depended on the belief in this 'reality' (e.g. the notion of the body, of the duration of substance, etc.). The sciences only prolong the process by means of which the essence of the species has been constructed, by making the belief in certain things endemic and by eliminating those who do not believe. The achieved similarity of sensation (concerning space, the sensation of time or the feeling of size) has become a condition for the existence of the species, but it has nothing to do with truth. (9/500)

When Nietzsche says that the sciences are shadows of the dead God, he means to say that we ought not to understand our age as the result of a scientific spirit revolting against the Christian spirit. Rather he speaks of a victory of the Christian conscience against itself, of the Christian will to truth turning its sting against itself. Finally, this conscience 'forbids itself the lie of faith in God':

You see what has really triumphed over the Christian god: Christian morality itself, the concept of truthfulness that was understood ever more rigorously, the father confessor's refinement of the Christian conscience, translated and sublimated into a scientific conscience, into intellectual cleanliness at any price. (GS 307)

Against this victory of Christian conscience, Nietzsche speaks of his desire to ' *"naturalize"* humanity in terms of a pure, newly discovered, newly redeemed nature' (GS 169). Thus we can see that this nature has little to do with that which we nowadays call 'nature'. As he argued in *Human, All too Human*, when Kant speaks of us as prescribing the law to nature, then this is correct with respect to the concept of nature. But this concept, since Descartes, is the idea of a world as we represent it to ourselves, which is to say, an error (2/41). This world is the sum of a lot of misunderstandings, of anthropomorphisms, of understanding something by means of turning it into its opposite. Strangely enough, Nietzsche can thus claim that in the age of the natural sciences we are further apart from nature than ever before.

iv. THE MEANING OF 'THE CRITICAL PHASE'

In our considerations of philosophical thinking and education, we have already seen that it would be quite a mistake to separate Nietzsche's writings into three different phases thought of as so-called changes of mind and direction in his philosophical stance. Philosophy has to be a movement of thinking. It is in this sense that Nietzsche identifies three stages in his thought which he calls those of the camel, the lion and the child. Thus instead of understanding his work as a step from an artist's metaphysics to an embrace of science and a consecutive flight from this critique back into 'literature', the 'middle phase' of his writings is trying to achieve a critique of science, not by finding good arguments against it, but by following its logic as one of destruction. It is for this reason that the three works belonging to this 'phase', *Human, All too Human, Dawn* and *The Gay Science*, are all fraught with contradiction. This phase is often called his 'positivistic' phase, but what is often overlooked is that this positivism of science is, for Nietzsche, a transitory stance.

Nietzsche gives us another clear outline of his own philosophical development by means of an account of the task of philosophy generally within the framework of its history. Here European history is described as the 'history of an error', in which 'the real world finally becomes a myth' (TI 20). The subtitle of this work, 'How to Philosophize with a Hammer', makes it quite clear that Nietzsche is still struggling with his positive philosophy; that is to say, that he still attempts to rid himself finally of the modern style of criticism. In this passage, Nietzsche recounts the story of Western metaphysics from Plato to nineteenth-century scepticism in four steps, supplemented by the two steps that his own philosophy is supposed to accomplish. That this is *one* history in six steps reinforces Nietzsche's understanding of European history as the history of philosophy. To see himself as overturning Platonism, then, means to become the inheritor of this metaphysics, and, at the same time, its end. The first three steps bridge the history of philosophy from Plato, via Christian theology to Kant, while the fourth step describes the beginning of positivism, followed by the characterization of Nietzsche's own stance as taken in *Human, All too Human.*

4. The real world – unattainable? Unattained, at any rate. And if unattained also *unknown*. Consequently also no consolation, no redemption, no duty: how could we have a duty towards something unknown?
(The grey of dawn. First yawnings of reason. Cockcrow of positivism.)

5. The 'real world' – an idea no longer of any use, not even a duty any longer – an idea grown useless, superfluous, *consequently* a refuted idea: let us abolish it!
(Broad daylight; breakfast; return of cheerfulness and *bon sens*; Plato blushes for shame; all free spirits run riot.) (TI 20)

While many commentators have understood Nietzsche's position in the 'critical phase' to constitute a wholehearted embrace of positivism following on his disappointment with Wagner, we have already seen that this phase is envisaged at the beginning of his work under the title of 'knowledge turning its sting against itself', that is, as a destructive movement, here called a philosophizing with a hammer. In this sense it does not depend on details of scientific research, nor does Nietzsche import scientific concepts or results into philosophy. Instead the books in question investigate the clash between science and morality following the collapse of the supersensuous realm – that is, the death of God. In this sense they are a preparation for the thought of the *Eternal Return of the Same*, which, after all, had been brooding in Nietzsche for a few years and became explicit in his thinking in 1881. As Nietzsche makes clear, Christian theology and the modern sciences belong together like mountain and valley, or rather, like the true world and the world of appearance, and in this sense they are both to be understood as 'Platonism for the people'. Nietzsche's thought thus only begins properly with the sixth step in the 'History of an Error':

> 6. We have abolished the real world: what world is left? The apparent world perhaps? . . . But no! *With the real world we have also abolished the apparent world!*
> (Mid-day; moment of the shortest shadow; end of the longest error; zenith of mankind; INCIPIT ZARATHUSTRA.)

In other words: our modern age believes in the givenness of a world conceived according to a Platonic or Christian idea, in which we no longer believe. Hence, insofar as we believe in science, we believe in something which we have at the same time made incredible. We therefore believe in something out of which we have made nothing. Insofar as Nietzsche is concerned, this means that we believe in the apparent world, while, *'with the real world we have also abolished the apparent world'* (TI 20). Once again, in other words – which Nietzsche uses in *The Gay Science*, in the famous paragraph entitled 'The Madman' – we have killed God, or the real world, without realizing what this means, namely without realizing that we have hence destroyed the apparent world which we were trying to save.

It is in this context that we can make sense of the 'positivist' phase of Nietzsche's thought. Being aware of its destructive nature, we will not be surprised by the infinite contradictions between the various arguments made in these books. It is strange to read the subtitle of *Human, All too Human*, namely 'A Book for Free Spirits', considering that it apparently denies the existence of free spirits. You only have to look at Book II, 'On the History of the Moral Sensations': 'everything here is necessary, every motion mathematically calculable. The actor's deception regarding himself, the assumption of free will, is itself part of this calculable mechanism' (HAH 57).

The 'Book for Free Spirits' claims that there is no such thing as freedom of choice, that it is hence a mere illusion if I think that I am free to do this or something totally different. Well, while we are not free, we are at least freed, namely freed from all guilt. *Human, All too Human* advocates the teaching of total irresponsibility. If there is no difference between the true world and the world of appearances, then we ought to be able to compare natural and human phenomena: ' *"Man's actions are always good"* – We do not accuse nature of immorality when it sends us a thunderstorm and makes us wet: why do we call the harmful man immoral? Because in the latter case we assume a voluntarily commanding free will, in the former necessity. But this distinction is an error' (HAH § 102). And, four sections later: *'By the waterfall.* – At the sight of a waterfall we think we see in the countless curvings, twistings and breakings of the waves capriciousness and freedom of will; but everything here is necessary, every motion mathematically calculable. So it is too in the case of human actions' (HAH § 106).

We can see in the language of *Human, All too Human* the beginning of this movement in which knowledge turns its sting against itself. Precisely because knowledge does not concern mere ideas that could be invoked independently from history, the analysis of nihilism necessitates an antidote. The philosopher Friedrich Nietzsche sees himself as the physician of modern culture, who attempts a cure by pushing the illness through its paces, and who realizes that nihilism can only be healed by going through nihilism. That is why we can see in *Human, All too Human*, in *Dawn*, and in *The Gay Science*, a therapeutic interpretation by way of a movement from religion and art, those spiritual powers that Nietzsche praised six years earlier, back to the ethos of the natural sciences. Scepticism is not a belief that Nietzsche takes to be true or correct; rather the 'probable victory of scepticism' (HAH I, 1/21, 23) is a historical fact, to which philosophy will have to find an answer.

Nietzsche claims that he has freed himself, that he remains victorious, in a work which gives the impression that freedom is an illusion, that it is impossible to possess oneself, while stating, at the same time, that we all belong in the realm of a calculable mechanism. Here the value of thought has been diminished to such a degree that philosophy itself would become meaningless. So how can we then speak of the victory of Nietzsche, rather than of his disappearance in the indifferent field of natural necessity? To find an answer to this question, you just have to think of what he is doing here. One could once win by proving that there is a God, that there is something like human freedom, which would consequently ground the idea of human dignity. But God is dead and one's victory would be infinitely greater if one would be able to pass oneself over to the realm of necessity – inside of which this freedom could first of all become meaningful – without vanishing in it. This is the only way to reconcile the world with the human being, the only way to reach the essence of real philosophy. Compare the following citation from Schelling's *Essay on Human Freedom* from 1809, which could hardly make the point any more clearly:

> Without the contradiction of freedom and necessity not only philosophy but every nobler ambition of the spirit would sink to that death which is peculiar to those sciences in which that contradiction serves no function. To withdraw from the conflict by forswearing reason looks more like flight than victory. Another person would have the same right to turn his back on freedom in order to throw himself into the arms of reason and necessity, without there being any cause for self-congratulation on either side. (*Freedom* 9)

If there is any possible reason for self-congratulation, then it is given in the case that the human being can prove itself in the face of the discovery of the aimless and hence chaotic nature of the universe, without trying to find any salvation through the Christian belief in a better world, but rather finding the resources for life through the inner strength of affirmation. As that decision will be the outcome of our present age, Nietzsche can say that, since the death of God, we all belong to a *higher* history. This is a higher history because in looking at science from the perspective of life, it reintroduces history into our understanding of the world. The interest in physics, the cry of 'long live physics', is thus motivated by the search for this identity of freedom and necessity, by the attempt to see life as art:

> We, however, *want to become those we are* – human beings who

119

are new, unique, incomparable, who give themselves laws, who create themselves. To that end we must become the best learners and discoverers of everything that is lawful and necessary in the world: we must become *physicists* in order to be able to be *creators* in this sense . . . (GS 266)

v. GOOD AND BAD SCIENCE: THE ART OF GENEALOGY

Nietzsche has thus shown the nihilistic essence of the modern sciences. These divorce us from the creative essence of nature inasmuch as they divorce us from our living body. This reality of the living body would require us to pay attention to our sensations and to the perspective of sensation, rather than reducing knowledge to mathematical fact. He thus concludes that 'reality does not appear at all' in these sciences, 'not even as a problem', insofar as they are mere elaborations of logic and 'that applied logic, mathematics' (6/75). Given that we often think of the natural sciences as empirical, this critique sounds odd, but we need only think of the development of quantum mechanics in the twentieth century to see that the reduction of method to statistics ends up in a system of science which does not even allow for a representation in terms of sensation. When Heisenberg, for example, speaks of eleven dimensions, one might respond with fantasies of an enriched experience, but these dimensions are merely mathematical and not open to any possible experience whatsoever. It is for this reason that there is a contradiction in contemporary science, in that, as Heisenberg adds, the scientist has to be able to enter the laboratory in such a way that the world appears open to experience – that he can look through a microscope as if he was merely investigating an object – while quantum mechanics tells him that this is an erroneous position. This is the smallest possible residuum of sensation in contemporary science, which otherwise has worked out the notion of objectivity to such a degree that it lays claim to absolute truth, independent from any perspective. But to look at the world from such a perspectiveless perspective is meaningless and, as Nietzsche says, violates the very idea of the eye.

But if in the 'sciences', as far as we know them, 'reality does not even appear as a problem', what then are these good sciences, which Nietzsche speaks about? He gives us an answer in section 59 of *The Antichrist*:

What we have won back for ourselves today with an unspeakable amount of self-constraint . . . the free view of reality, the cautious hand, patience and seriousness in the smallest things, the whole *integrity* of knowledge – was already there! already more than two millennia ago! *And* good and delicate taste and tact! . . . *as body, as gesture, as instinct – in a word, as reality.* (AC 192)

Body, gesture, instinct: these are all involved perspectives; they are, 'in a word, . . . reality', precisely because they are not perspectives looking at the world as from above, but are looking from the inside. And it is precisely for this reason that they embody a 'higher objectivity', as they are no longer reducing the world to a universal form of human subjectivity, but take it as it appears by itself. It is thus that Nietzsche can say that we have a science today precisely insofar as we accept the witness of the senses and that we sharpen these senses. Such a science Nietzsche has found in the works of the Presocratic writers. If we read there, for example, a description of the movement of the sun from sunrise to sunset, then the result seems to us absurd, while there is nothing added to what one can see.

Such a science of the body, of gesture and instinct, is an artistic science in that it attempts to give credence to the way that things have become what they are. What for Hegel thus was a phenomenology of spirit, as paying attention to the historical reality of human existence, has become, for Nietzsche, a genealogy of the body. This no longer projects the truths of logic and rationality onto the world, but proceeds from the assumption that history is motivated by errors and accidents. In order to look for a truth in history one has to realize that 'the reason for the emergence of a thing and its ultimate usefulness, its factual utilization and integration into a system of ends are infinitely separated' (5/313).

God is dead, but religion and art have been those powers which *give* existence an eternal and stable character, which can thus sustain this character as they still harbour its becoming, while our modern natural sciences, pretending that the real essence of all things consists in their adherence to the laws of eternal truth, misunderstand both being and becoming. Nietzsche's critique of Christianity is thus not that it has given such an appearance to reality, while we should accept that there is none. Indeed, Nietzsche expresses his main critique of Christianity as having lost its artistic powers. 'Two millennia nearly', he says, 'and not a single new god' (5/185). The problem of the natural sciences is thus that they think of such eternal character of existence as something merely given in the notion of reason, while this reason is the worldly appearance of the dead God. Misunderstanding being and becoming means equally to misunderstand the notion of observation with respect to the powers of the eternal, and it is for this reason that science sees art and religion as hostile powers (HL 62). While science thus determines that which is already given – and it is for this reason that Nietzsche says that the sciences are Christian and nihilistic – art uncovers the possible within the world.

> This requires above all a great artistic capacity, and creative overview, a loving immersion in the empirical data, a poetic elaboration of given types – this, to be sure, requires objectivity, but as a positive property. Objectivity, however, is so often only a phrase. The dark tranquillity of the artist's eye, flashing within yet unmoved without, is replaced by the affectation of tranquillity; as lack of pathos and moral strength usually disguises itself as penetrating coolness of observation. In certain cases banality of sentiment and everyday wisdom, which by being so boring give the impression of tranquillity and calm, dare to step forth and pretend to be that artistic condition in which the subject is silent and becomes quite imperceptible. Then all those items which do not arouse at all are searched out and the dullest word is just right (HL § 6, p. 36f).

Nietzsche saw the signs of his time, and he thus saw that the fate of Western civilization would lead it, inescapably and with a remorseless necessity, into nihilism. The word nihilism stems from the Latin word *nihil*, meaning 'nothing'; nihilism hence denotes the belief in nothing; or, even worse, it describes the state of 'desiring nothing'. The form that this 'desiring nothing' takes in our age is called science. Nietzsche has consequently been described as the thinker of nihilism; yet that does not mean that he personally believed in nothing; nor that he did not believe in anything, but that he first of all grasped that nihilism is the inevitable fate of Western humanity, and that the task of philosophy thus consists in the understanding and overcoming of this nihilism.

In other words, insofar as nihilism is seen as a historical fact,

Nietzsche belongs to the age of nihilism, and he is too much of a thinker to claim that one could simply deny this state in that one believed in something else. And yet, as far as Nietzsche believes that through philosophical thinking, understood as the unity of philology and medicine, nihilism can be overcome, he is not a nihilist. In a letter of 23 May 1887, Nietzsche writes about the Swiss historian Burkhard, the French philosopher Taine, and himself:

> We are indeed and essentially dependent on each other, we three nihilists: although, I myself, as you might have felt, have not yet despaired of finding the exit and the hole through which one might be able to get to 'some-thing'. (KSA-B 8/81)

To get back to such a 'some-thing', Nietzsche develops three teachings, those of the *Overhuman*, of the *Eternal Return of the Same* and of the *Will to Power*. We are now in a position to turn to these.

CHAPTER 4

THE ETERNAL RETURN OF THE SAME

When in Infinity the Same
Eternally flows in repetition
When the variegated vault
Firmly closes up upon itself
Love of Living emanates from all things
The littlest and the grandest star
And all the straining, all the striving
Is eternal peace in God

The doctrine of the *Eternal Return of the Same* is, next to the *Will to Power*, the central thought of Nietzsche's philosophy. While he speaks of an epiphany of this thought while walking in the Alps in Summer 1881, it is not difficult to find various appearances of thoughts of recurrence in all his early writings, even in his juvenilia. Indeed, reading through Nietzsche's works in their chronological order one can see that this thought rises within him slowly, to come to fruition towards the end of his 'critical phase'. It is this experience of thinking which later finds expression in Zarathustra's slow apprehension of *Eternal Recurrence* in allegories which stress the affective character of thinking. Thus Zarathustra calls up this thought and is struck down by it. Similarly, when Nietzsche speaks of himself as a destiny and concludes that with him the history of mankind is struck asunder, then the meaning of these statements is to be found in the thought of the *Eternal Return of the Same*. This thought he calls the heaviest weight, bearing on European humankind as its most essential crisis – and

a crisis is a moment of decision, a moment that makes a difference.

Having destroyed, in the books of his 'middle period', all current
beliefs and convictions, culminating in the *Death of God*, it is this
thought of the *Eternal Return of the Same* that encourages him
to leave the 'lion phase' of *Human, All too Human, Dawn* and *The
Gay Science* behind. With this thought the trajectory of his own
thinking takes on shape and meaning; in short, Nietzsche now
comes to know who he is. Having wrestled with the form that thinking can take for him, with a style which would allow a concrete
philosophical intervention, Nietzsche now develops a renewed confidence in the future of his thought. The first book published after
this revelation of the *Eternal Return of the Same*, *The Gay Science*
from 1882, is already marked by this change. It is more decisive,
more directly structured and ends, considering that the fifth book
was added a few years later, with the first explicit elaboration of the
thought of *Eternal Recurrence*, followed by the annunciation: 'Thus
Zarathustra began to go under'. This going under refers to Zarathustra leaving his retreat in the mountains in order to return to
the society of human beings, there to become the teacher of the
Eternal Return of the Same and the *Overhuman*.

We have already encountered the figure of a teaching in
Nietzsche's thought and we know by now that it is not sufficient to
consider this abstractly as an idea. A teaching directs itself at the
very being of the teacher and the pupil, which is also to say that,
depending on who we are, we are going to understand it differently,
while this understanding is, again, not given in the form of 'correct
belief', but in terms of the change in one's being, having undergone
the thought. To say that in simpler terms, a teaching, in order to be
successful, has to pick us up where we are, and has to develop right
through the process of the incorporation of this thought. In the
case of the thought of *Eternal Recurrence*, this means that we have
to begin with the human being of our contemporary age, to confront it with this thought and thus to make it understand that the
human being has come to an end. The crisis appearing from this
confrontation, from the inability to bear this thought, is described
by Zarathustra as developing either backwards towards the animal
or forwards towards the *Overhuman* (10/479).

What does this mean? We just have to bear in mind that Nietzsche
uses words in a concrete sense. Thus the 'human being' is for him

not a biological category, meaning *homo sapiens* or *biped*, but the historical form of the self-interpretation of human existence that we call Platonism. According to this understanding, the human being is the halfway house between heaven and earth, which is to say, in more contemporary terms, that we understand ourselves in terms of the opposition between an animal body and a divine mind. All our convictions and instincts with respect to action, being, knowing, and to institutions, whether these be legal, political or cultural, are derived from this essential self-interpretation that Nietzsche calls history. Insofar as he called this history equally philosophy or European Nihilism, the end of it concerns our nihilism, that is, our inability to value our existence in a meaningful sense. In other words, the *Death of God* has made belief in our divine part impossible, so that this has become the abstract and indifferent idea of scientific representation.

Since the great error of Descartes, consisting in the substantial separation of thought from the world of objects, we have thought of truth as a representation of the world in the form of ideas. In Descartes we have found the conception of the modern scientific world-picture. When, in the Sixth Meditation, Descartes argues that we can understand the world in the abstraction of final causes, he gives rise to an understanding of nature as merely mechanical. Herewith the notion of the world as necessary causation stands in opposition to the notion of the human mind and its freedom. This 'mind–body' problem has led during the course of the Enlightenment to an incompatibility between our experience of human freedom, on the one hand, and the progressively successful methods of the natural sciences, on the other.

It is quite simple: if we think of the role of the body as pure mechanism, having since Descartes counted animals as belonging purely to this mechanism, while no longer being able to believe in the divine part that, according to modernity, has made the difference between animal and human being, then we end up with a human being which can no longer see its difference from other animals and hence develops back into animal life. When Nietzsche talked in the *Twilight of the Idols* about the abolition of the true world, then the human being that we are still understands itself with respect to this loss, namely inhabiting solely the appearing world, not realizing that this world too has already been implicitly abolished. This animal might be clever and develop sciences and sustained technological progress, yet the fundamental interpretation of this progress again reduces the human being to a calculative machine, so that all this knowledge fails to make an essential difference. This is why Zarathustra says: 'But he who is wizest among you, he also is only a discord and hybrid of plant and ghost' (Z 42). Equally, we are putting more and more stress on education, which Nietzsche identified as a practice of breeding, but we tend today to reduce this to an information transfer equipping us for the economic world, without making an essential difference with respect to ourselves. The analogy that we often hear about today, which likens the mind and its knowledge to the difference in computers between hardware and software, makes this quite clear, insofar as the software is understood as making no difference to the hardware. In other words, we think of such information as fact, and of our capacity to deal with information as yet another fact.

The relation between the self-interpretation of our being and the truth of our being can be further illuminated if we think of the inspiration of rationalism on Nietzsche's thinking. Leibniz, Spinoza and Hegel have shown in different ways that what we know is intrinsically related to who we are. Hegel, especially, has demonstrated this identity between thought and being by way of its historical mediation. Insofar as Nietzsche has radicalized this notion of history, he has shown that there are no eternal truths, and that this also holds for the essence of the human being. There is thus no real fact concerning our essence. Consequently, when Nietzsche first experiences the revelation of the thought of the *Eternal Return of the Same* in 1881, this thought brings with it the insight into the 'infinite importance of our knowledge, our errors, of our habits and ways of life for all that is to come' (9/494).

While the notion of a 'mind–body' problem in Descartes remains relatively abstract, the Kantian formulation of this problem remains, for Nietzsche, more essential. Again, Nietzsche is not very interested in deciding whether Kant is right or wrong, but in how the Kantian problematic most clearly outlines the essential way in which we interpret our own existence through the schism between theoretical and practical knowledge, which is to say, between ontology and ethics. Kant is the first European philosopher who successfully accounts for the knowledge of our world without reference to divine creation. Insofar as there is, consequently, nothing in this world which escapes our knowledge, he can construct the idea of the world in its full objectivity. And yet this world, insofar as we understand it, leaves no space for human freedom. The latter Kant conceives in relation to the categorical imperative, which is to say to a voice that speaks to us from outside of the world of objects. The world which we know does not allow for any intuition of freedom, necessary for any formulation of morality, and therefore the voice calling us to do the good has to come from outside of the world we know, which is to say, from God. In this respect, Kant is quite clear about the problem, which he outlines at the beginning of his third critical work, the *Critique of Judgement*, namely that both these 'worlds' of necessity and freedom are mutually exclusive. Insofar as the world that we understand scientifically must be free from any effects of freedom, freedom cannot be apparent in it, while any notion of freedom remains completely vain unless it can bear an effect in the world itself.

This is the historical foundation of European Nihilism, and it clarifies the beginning of the teaching of the *Eternal Return of the Same*. Recalling that Nietzsche calls the philosopher a physician, we just have to remind ourselves that the first step in the process of healing is the recognition of the illness itself. Without such recognition there can be no healing. But why do we not see the problem, as Nietzsche does, in Kantianism? Did we not just say that Kant was quite aware of it when writing the introduction to the *Third Critique*? Yes, but it seems to appear there as a 'logical problem'. Insofar as Kant accounted for the essence of the human being in transcendental terms, it is understood there as an eternal truth, which is also to say as an inalienable possession, in the same sense as we still speak today about human rights as inalienable possessions. One thus need not do anything about this problem but wait until somebody comes up with the answer. The teaching of *Eternal Recurrence*, on the other hand, is to make the suffering palpable to us, or, as Nietzsche says, unbearable. Once it has become the greatest weight lying on any of our decisions, it will have an effect, namely our insight into our illness, into that which Nietzsche early on called the *historical malady*, and later, European Nihilism.

But if this is the case, we can immediately see that the thought of *Eternal Recurrence* has to bear this contradiction within itself. It will have to begin with two faces contradicting each other: one of these standing for our interpretation of the world, one for our interpretation of human freedom. Insofar as the first answers the question 'What is the world?' we call it the 'ontological' or the 'cosmological' thesis of the *Eternal Return of the Same*. Insofar as the second answers the question 'What ought I to do?' we call it the 'ethical' thesis of the *Eternal Return of the Same*. We are thus guarding ourselves from the error that many commentators fall into when they ask whether Nietzsche meant the thought of *Eternal Recurrence* either as an ethical thought or as an interpretation of the world itself. At the outset this thought has to be both, and thus bring out their contradiction. That is why Nietzsche says that this thought brings together 'the two most extreme ways of thinking – the mechanical and the platonic' (WP 1061). By following this sentence with the claim that *Eternal Recurrence* brings these out as ideals, rather than as real, historical interpretations, we will easily make the error of thinking that only one of them can be true, unless we realize that truth itself is here at stake.

i. THE ONTOLOGICAL FACE OF THE *ETERNAL RETURN OF THE SAME*

The ontological or cosmological version of the *Eternal Return of the Same* thus attempts to think through the mechanistic world view and to bring out its truth. To call it a world view is slightly misleading, as it concerns not only our beliefs or opinions, but our very being. Thus the beginning of the thought is given by Nietzsche when saying that our *sensations*, not just our conceptions, of space and time lead us into the error of nihilism.

But to put our sensations of the world into question is something nearly impossible to do. We can certainly discuss the validity of ideas, but the validity of perceptions seems to be beyond questioning. Or the sceptic might question whether my representations of the world are related to an actual world out there or whether, like dream images, they are only fictional, but he cannot question that they are as they are. The German word for perception shows this point clearly, insofar as *Wahrnehmung* literally means 'taking [for] true'. Therefore Nietzsche cannot argue about the correctness or incorrectness of our perceptions, but he can demonstrate that the way that we perceive the world has certain consequences, namely that it leads us into nihilism. For this he has only to go to the root of our fundamental understanding of the world to derive the thought of *Eternal Recurrence* as a consequence of the way that we think and experience the world.

It is thus from the outset quite clear that the thought of the *Eternal Return of the Same* is not a scientific thought and that it cannot be in any way verified or falsified by scientific experiments or 'data'. Rather it is a thought that attempts to make us understand the very basis of the modern natural sciences, a basis which holds sway over all our thinking and feeling, even of those who are not at all interested in physics, biology or chemistry. But what is the essence of our understanding of the world? As we have already encountered this question in the last chapter, I will here only repeat the essentials.

Since Descartes has eradicated the idea of final causation from our understanding of nature, this nature appears to us as the mere sum of all objects in motion. It is understood by what we loosely call materialism, i.e. there are extended objects and every present conjunction of such objects can be understood as the effect of a past conjunction of objects and their motion. These objects move in space and they move through time. Time and space are thereby conceived of as infinite magnitudes, which is to say that they do not begin or end anywhere and that they are indifferent to what happens 'in' them. That I can measure the movement of atoms or of stars by way of a clock and a meter is due to the conviction that time and space are constant, i.e. that they are not subject to change, that I can measure any movement against them. In this sense we experience time as an infinite sequence of now points and space as an infinity of mathematical points which we can represent as three-dimensional against an x, y, and z axis. Insofar as these thus have the character of universal necessity, and as something universal cannot be derived from experience, Kant demonstrates that time and space are *a priori* intuitions and can thus be understood absolutely independently from experience as the foundations of arithmetic, insofar as the intuition of time furnishes the 1+1+1 . . . lying at the origin of number, and geometry, insofar as its axioms are given in the intuition of space.

Leibniz and Newton add to this formulation of nature that its substance is not to be explained by extension, but by the concept of force. But how does this notion of force as the substance of nature inform our experience of it? A force is not a thing, which is to say that it cannot be understood as a single entity. Rather every force is equal to its expression and can thus be understood only in its relation to other forces. Thus Newton says that to every force corresponds a contrary force of equal measure, while the sum total of all forces is therefore always identical with itself. This is called the law of the conservation of force. And we can see already that a force, as quantifiable, can be fully determined mathematically. Thus, Nietzsche says, where there is force there is also number, and where there is number there is also finitude. The sum total of all forces might be beyond our faculty of representation, but it is, nonetheless, in principle finite; that is, the amount of forces might be innumerable, but it is not infinite. In the following Nietzsche will demonstrate that this law of the conservation of energy calls for the *Eternal Recurrence* (12/205).

From here the thought of the *Eternal Return of the Same* follows quite clearly: we understand the world as the play of a finite set of forces, so that every now point can be understood as the 'frozen' image of the relation of all given forces to each other at a given moment. This we might call the now-state of all forces. Insofar as we understand any given now as the causal consequence of the preceding now, we also call this the sum total of all facts, insofar as 'facts' are by definition states which find their meaning in their causal past. The world understood as becoming, as engendering itself from a process of the determination of forces, of dynamical quanta, is in consequence also necessarily finite, the more so as the law of the conservation of energy demands that the overall sum of force is always identical. Yet something finite, engendering itself in infinite time, must necessarily repeat itself *ad infinitum*.

Let us for the moment think of this in terms of playing with dice, representing the state of a force by the number shown on a dice and the now-state of all forces with the sum of all dice. Let us say we play with twenty billion dice, then any possible combination of numbers stands for a possible relation of all forces making up the world. The sum total of all different combinations is, obviously, quite enormous, but it can easily be calculated, which is to say, it is a finite number. Now the chance of throwing twenty billion sixes in one go is rather small, yet imagining that we would play *ad infinitum*, it will have to happen one day. Once it does happen, we start again, until it happens again, and again, and again. In short, if we had always played and never stop playing, then the throw of twenty billion sixes will not only have happened a lot of times, not even innumerably many times, but it will already have happened infinite times and will again happen infinite times. Thus an infinite number of states of forces (*Kraftlagen*) has already passed in infinite time, precisely because an infinite amount of nows has already passed, yet 'not an infinite number of *different* states', insofar as that would 'presuppose an undetermined force', while force is by definition determined by number, i.e. by a finitude of different characteristics (9/530).

But why should it be impossible that a finite number of elements could generate an infinite number of qualitatively different states of forces? Prior to the establishment of the modern scientific world-picture we might have believed that there had to be an infinite force in order to explain the infinite sequence of events in the world. As there seemed to be no beginning of motion and no end, its explan-ation seemed to require a force 'which cannot be exhausted by its expenditure' (9/544). This infinite force was called God, who was thus able to create the world out of nothing. Yet with the *Death of God* – that is, with the impossibility of belief in a world beyond this world – we see force as always remaining the same. God as infinite quantum, which is to say, as quality, would have been able to create an always different world, insofar as he creates out of nothing, while the world, conceived of from the vantage point of science, might be 'infinitely active, but it can no longer create infinite cases, it has to repeat itself' (9/544). Nietzsche thus concludes:

> In which judgement or belief can we best express the decisive turn being engendered by the preponderance of the spirit of science over the religious, Gods-creating spirit? We insist that the world, as force, is not to be thought of as unlimited – we forbid the concept of an infinite force as incompatible with the concept 'force'. (9/575)

Here the analogy with playing dice has its limitations. Calculating the chances of throwing a certain combination of numbers, the purely logical amount of different combinations is also the actual count of combinations in statistical variation. The second step of the argument then has to differentiate itself from the example, prov-ing that states of the differential of forces are dependent on each other through time, i.e. that they are not produced by chance. This necessary link between two different states of forces is what we call causality. Insofar as the becoming of the world is understood as the explication of forces, one moment is seen as the consequence of the moment preceding it, while it necessarily draws another moment after it.

Consequently the cycle of all events does not close itself after all logical possibilities have become actual. Indeed, the number of logical possibilities necessarily exceeds the number of actualities. We can clarify this again with the example of dice. Let us assume we only throw one dice. We start by throwing a six, followed by a three, a five and a two, after which we again throw a six. As we now posit that from a six necessarily follows a three, then a five and then a two, we have established that the logical possibilities of throwing a one or a four are impossible actualities.

But why should this point be of any consequence? Consider how one looks at the world as it is and one tries to counter its shortcomings by the idea of progress, conceived of in its telos by way of what we call a utopian state of affairs. Like the Christian, one might say that this world is the 'valley of tears', but that it will come to an end, insofar as we can aim for making this utopia a reality, namely by passing the test of existence so that we pass into a meaningful afterlife. Like the revolutionary, one might say that history up to today has been a meaningless and cruel sequence of human suffering and exploitation, while we can conceive of a state of justice. This ideal state he thus proposes as a utopia which we might attempt to realize through political action. One would thus be able to escape the consequences of the *Eternal Return of the Same* by way of believing that the world could be moved by mere ideals. Generally speaking, any idea of a utopia and of progress in this sense, which, like the Enlightenment, thinks of establishing the reign of reason in this world, remains for Nietzsche an idealism which, while proclaiming to wish to make the world a better place, is really animated by a resentment against life, thereby unwittingly devaluing life.

But, in any case, these remain arguments open to discussion, while Nietzsche attempts to demonstrate that, immanent to the way that we experience the world, we have already given up on any such utopia. In other words, it is true that we can account logically for the possibility of a final, perfect state of the world, but conceived from the perspective of *Eternal Recurrence*, such logical possibility shows itself to be actually impossible. If such a final state was possible, it would already have been reached in the infinite past and, if it was final and perfect, it would have persisted. As it has not been reached, it is shown to be logically possible, but actually impossible. The consequence is that it cannot be left to the human mind to determine what is *possible* (9/534), an argument which brings into question the whole idea of an active, logical mind confronting a passive world of mere data.

While this conception of *Eternal Recurrence* thinks through the consequences of our mechanistic world-picture, it equally shows its limitations. As Nietzsche says, mechanism implies a purpose, which would be achieved as the final end of this mechanism. Yet such an end has not been reached and is therefore impossible (WP 1066). To escape such conclusion, one often thinks of the becoming of the universe in analogy with that of an organism, a living whole. Nietzsche counters this idea with the argument that the cosmos cannot be an organism, insofar as an organism is always dependent on something outside. The world cannot be thought of organically, as any organism depends on a world.

> The idea of an infinite becoming of the new is a contradiction. It would presuppose an infinitely growing force. But from what should it grow! From what should it nourish itself, nourish itself with a surplus! The assumption that the cosmos is an organism contradicts the notion of the organic. (9/525)

But what is the point of this argument? Maybe it becomes clearer if we return briefly to Hegel's idea of the world spirit. As we have seen in our reflections on history, Hegel's argument concerning historical becoming also uses the figure of the circle. And yet, returning to itself, spirit develops further in that it takes this development up into itself in the form of a historical memory. *Absolute Spirit* was then the recollection of all pasts into the presence of its world. Such an idea of history would allow us to escape the consequences of the teaching of the *Eternal Return of the Same*, insofar as every cycle would incorporate the last and, indeed, all those preceding it. The world would thus, while repeating itself, continuously create something new.

The implications of the *Eternal Return of the Same* are, on the contrary, analogous to contemporary representations of the Big Bang–Big Crunch theory of the universe. Here we often hear that time begins with the Big Bang and ends with the Big Crunch, but to put it this way is slightly misleading. Insofar as the Big Bang is thought of as an event, it is thought in time, so that there is a before and an after. Yet, insofar as the matter emerging from the Big Bang does not bear any memory of any preceding event which could be conceived of as its cause, one says that there is no trace of a temporal development, which is to say that all considerations of time as the sequence of the causal chain start at that very moment. It is thus only this causal chain which is thought to begin here. In other words, we can follow back the physical development through time only insofar as we can go back through the causal chain, yet in the Big Bang this chain has been severed.

It is thus not the case that the Hegelian idea of absolute spirit is directly equivalent with that of an organic life form, but they agree in that absolute spirit equally develops in taking everything up into itself and thus at any stage creates something new in the form of a being with a new past. Yet, as we have seen, the idea of the universe as an organism is incompatible with the idea of the organic:

> inorganic matter, although having most of the time been organic, has learned nothing, is always without past! If this was not so, then there could never be any repetition – because there would always be the generation of something out of material with new qualities, with new pasts. (9/578)

A finite world that moves 'inside' an infinite time cannot be conceived except as having already been innumerable times and as returning again innumerable times. We are now in a position to understand Nietzsche's summary of the ontological version of *Eternal Recurrence*:

> The new Conception of the World – *1. The world exists; she is nothing which becomes, nothing which vanishes. Or, rather: she becomes, she vanishes, but she never began to become and she never stopped to vanish – she subsists through both . . .*
>
> 5. If it is allowed to think the world as a determined amount of force and as a determined number of centres of forces – and indeed, any other idea of the world remains undetermined and thus useless – then we have to conclude that, in the great dice game of her existence, there is a calculable number of different

possible combinations which she has to pass through. In infinite
time each possible combination would once be reached; or rather:
it would infinite times have been reached. And as all possible
combinations must have taken place between each 'combination'
and its next 'return', and as each of these combinations causes
the whole sequence of combinations in the same order, we thus
proved a circle of absolutely identical sequences: the world as a
circle, which has already repeated itself infinite times and which
plays its game *ad infinitum*. (WP 1066)

And yet, we have to bear in mind that this is not 'Nietzsche's theory', but the thinking through of our innermost convictions regarding the world of nature. Whenever we speak about 'nature or
nurture', about 'fact and value', about 'mind and body', about 'freedom and necessity', we give expression to this belief. Nietzsche does
not posit the infinity of a linear time forwards and backwards as a
scientific thesis. On the contrary, he argues that this is a flat and
erroneous conception of time. Neither could there be any scientific
proof for such a theory, as any scientific theory has already to presuppose these notions. Is this to say that this notion of time is
simply and necessarily true? No: instead we find the infinity of time
in the indifferent sequence of now-points as an event in the history
of the self-interpretation of European humankind.

The ontological version of the *Eternal Return of the Same* thus
ensues from the original thesis of the *Death of God* and the establishment of the modern natural sciences as the only access to truth.
We have suffered the death of the true world. What world is left?
The apparent world, the world of facts. What are the consequences
of this representation?

1. The different cycles are characterized by absolute determinacy,
    by stringent causality, and, as soon as the same state is produced
    a second time, a new cycle begins. There are two problems: a) as
    is well known, Nietzsche rejects all forms of determinism and
    causality as scientific simplifications or falsifications; b) inside
    of one cycle, as Nietzsche argues, it is impossible that the same
    state is produced. But if that is the case, then the closure of
    one cycle and thus the beginning of a new one become highly
    problematic, the schism between beginning and end disrupts
    the continuity of becoming. Only on a mechanistic premise

could the *Eternal Return of the Same* be represented as a program loop without exit or as an infinitely repeated movement from Big Bangs to Big Crunches. From the perspective of the *Eternal Return of the Same* there is no beginning nor end, rather the cycle begins and ends in every now. It is what gives the now its present, precisely insofar as it repeats itself.

2. In this *Eternal Return of the Same* nothing ever returns – or, rather, it makes no difference that everything returns as the same. With the same argument – at least with regards to its form – which Nietzsche used against the possible actualization of an equilibrium of forces, he counters that inside of one cycle, diachronically as well as synchronically, there could be two 'things' characterized by sameness (9/523, 530). That there is sameness for us is simply due to the laziness, the habitual nature of our fantasy (9/493) and its falsifications for the sake of creating the most adequate conditions for life.

3. Nothing returns – because nothing can ever have existed in an original mode, i.e. for the first time, preceding any repetition. In short, nobody produced the model of which all subsequent repetitions are the copies. As far backwards into infinity as one can think, there was always already another cycle preceding the cycle in question. The innocence of becoming as the result of the fact that there was no doer behind the deed is *amor fati*: fatalism. The *Eternal Return of the Same* is hence characterized as pure repetition, not as representation of the cycle. We just have to remember that we are not looking at this cycle from the outside, but that *we* are and that this *thought* appears within the cycle. From this perspective, as we said before, the cycle begins and ends at any now.

4. Nothing returns – because the temporal distinction of two cycles breaks down. In other words, there is no means to distinguish between the actual repetition, its last, and its next instance. Either there is a numerical difference and a temporal distance – then what returns is obviously not the same – or difference and distance are inessential – then what returns is identical. From this point follows also that inside of history the same constellation of questions or problems never returns.

What does remain of this cosmological version of the *Eternal Return of the Same*? The two sides of this Platonism without God:

namely an explanation of how the scientific world-picture creates the appearance of being in our world – that is, how its interpretation of time is derived from Platonism – and, on the other hand, the insight that this world of modern science is nihilistic. There seems to be no sense in a world which returns and returns, where determinism is not only understood on account of individual scientific proofs of a correlation between human behaviour, on the one hand, and genes, hormones, chemicals, etc., on the other hand, but where one has shown that freedom and meaningful action are in principle impossible, before any proof or any argument.

Many commentators attempt to argue that Nietzsche did not really believe in the thought of the *Eternal Return of the Same* in an ontological sense. Some argue that Nietzsche wanted to furnish scientific proofs for the notion of *Eternal Recurrence*. We have now seen that both these positions are absurd. The first, because Nietzsche's task was precisely to bring out the essence of the world we live in, in order to demonstrate that it is, inescapably, nihilistic. The second, therefore, because it addresses itself to the very foundation of modern physics, to its very presuppositions, for which even the idea of proof is meaningless.

ii.   THE ETHICAL FACE OF THE *ETERNAL RETURN OF THE SAME*

We have seen that the cosmological version of *Eternal Recurrence* has led to the insight that life is impossible within the understanding of the world of the modern natural sciences. It brought out the consequences of the scientific world view, starting with the foundations of the modern sciences from their beginnings in Leibniz and Newton and from their formulation in the Kantian critical system which posits the incompatibility of theoretical and practical knowledge. But what of the other side, of the question of morality? Insofar as both theoretical and practical philosophy are still essentially Platonic, both in their content and their separation, the thought of *Eternal Recurrence* should be equally able to give us an understanding of modern morality. Insofar as the question of ethical action concerns the notion of a meaning or purpose which directs my action towards the future, the ethical version of the *Eternal Return of the Same* stands in direct contrast to the cosmological. Therefore we should expect that the ethical explanation will come to look a bit like the Kantian idea of morality.

Indeed, in terms of Nietzsche's published writings, the ethical explanation of *Eternal Recurrence* precedes the cosmological. Towards the end of the first version of *The Gay Science*, in section 341, Nietzsche gives expression to 'the greatest weight' in the following terms:

> What if some day or night a demon were to steal after you into your loneliest loneliness and say to you: 'This life as you now live it and have lived it, you will have to live once more and innumerable times more; and there will be nothing new in it, but every pain and every joy and every thought and sigh ... will have to return to you, all in the same succession and sequence – even this spider and this moonlight ... and even this moment and I myself'. (GS 273)

At first, it seems that we are here again confronted with the cosmological version of *Eternal Recurrence*, namely with the idea that human action is impossible, as it is fated to repeat in any case what is already given. And yet, we have already discussed the question of fatalism in the first chapter. There we have seen that the fatalist is the most active human being, precisely insofar as he cannot escape action. Nietzsche thus asks how one would respond to such a thought. One could despair and think that one cannot do anything, as everything has already been determined in advance, hence remaining passive, or one could grasp this thought as saying that anything I will do will have been done by necessity and will be repeated into eternity.

As we have seen with the ontological version of *Eternal Recurrence*, there cannot be any knowledge of what is necessary, precisely because there is no memory reaching from one repetition to the next. Thus everything becomes possible. Consequently the *Eternal Return of the Same* can become that thought which turns my otherwise arbitrary and unjustifiable action into something necessary and, therefore, justified.

The thought of *Eternal Recurrence* hence turns from looking backwards to looking forwards. That is to say, instead of saying that whatever I do is just a repetition of that which I have already done infinite times, I come to see that whatever I do now, I will do again and again into all future eternity. That is why this thought now comes to lie on all my decisions as the greatest weight: 'Do you want this again and again, infinite times?' (GS 341). The thought of the *Eternal Return of the Same* thus provides us with a formal criterion for any possible action, in a way analogous to the Kantian moral imperative. To have a short look at the latter will help us to develop Nietzsche's thought, especially as we know already that Nietzsche formulated the thought of *Eternal Recurrence* against Kantianism, considered not as a philosophical theory, but as giving expression to the nihilistic nature of our self-understanding in modernity.

The split between the transcendental constitution of the world and its empirical existence can easily be seen as the difference between a form, on the one hand, and matter, on the other. As to the discussion of the moral law, this means that Kant will not provide us with any table of dos and don'ts which impose themselves on the individual from the outside. Rather, the individual, from a feeling of respect for the moral law, is required by duty to represent herself as an individual with particular desires within the confines of this law, so as to find a formal rule by means of which she can judge an action as moral or immoral. Hereby a moral action is one that places me within the interests of the human community, while an immoral action is one that opposes the fulfilment of my own desires to this community. To take one example, charity belongs to that class of actions which supports the community as such, which reduces suffering and which I could ask anyone to look at as an example to follow. Stealing money, on the other hand, even if under special circumstances I could claim that it would reduce suffering, cannot be recommended to all as an example to follow, as it would erode the community as such. Kant thus does not give us a rule that can judge universally that 'charity is good', 'stealing is bad', etc., but he can give us a rule which we can apply to any possible action at any given point. This is called the categorical imperative. One of its formulations is the following: 'Act only according to that maxim by which you can at the same time will that it should become a universal law'. With regard to any particular act I am thus obliged to extrapolate its universal form, stipulating that as this form it ought to oblige everyone who would find herself in a similar situation.

But why would one have to stipulate that this form is not just a practical norm that I might or might not apply? In other words, why would Kant need to demonstrate that this norm goes back to a categorical imperative, a command obliging me unconditionally? The answer is quite simple. If it were only a practical norm that I might apply or not, I would not speak of morality in the sense of a moral law, but only about a personal inclination to orient myself in my practical concerns. This is why this moral conscience obliges me by way of a feeling, namely that of respect for the moral law as the foundation of human freedom. It is thus not self-will that motivates me, but the ideal will of all, and it is this which makes this a moral consideration, insofar as it is built on a feeling which exceeds my own thinking and, therefore, directs itself to my very being. Otherwise I might be able to attribute this thinking to the world of knowledge, but that is, as we have seen, devoid of any intuition of freedom. This is why Kant calls the moral law sublime, which is to say, exceeding my ability to understand it by means of representation. It is the starry sky above us and the infinity of the moral law within us which, as he says, command our respect.

In Nietzsche, this voice of God has been transformed into that of a demon: 'What if some day or night a demon were to steal after you into your loneliest loneliness . . .' This figure of the demon we already know from Descartes' *Meditations*, where it served as the idea of a creator God bereft of his benevolence, which is to say, bereft of his infinity. And this demon, too, was speaking to me in my loneliest loneliness, insofar as it was the idea of a God-creator who has created my world without allowing me to share this world with others. The demon here presents the idea of the categorical imperative after the *Death of God*. One might, then, reformulate the categorical imperative into the language of the *Eternal Return of the Same*: 'Act only according to that maxim by which you can at the same time will that it can become a law for all your eternity'; which is to say, 'Act thus that you can will this act again and again for all eternity'.

But we can see immediately that this is but a pale reflection of the categorical imperative. We could phrase this with an exaggeratedly banal example: as I was wondering whether I should lay waste to a few hours by watching television, the demon might persuade me that this would mean wasting an infinity of time, thus paying rather heavily for this negligence. But, whatever example one might take, we end up with a merely abstract thought, without any considerable force. Wondering whether I should stop smoking, because it might finally kill me, I silently respond 'No it won't'; wondering whether I should not waste those few hours, because they will return again and again, I respond silently, 'No, they won't really and, in any case, even if they might, I will be completely oblivious to that'. As we have found again and again with Nietzsche, he argues stringently that abstract logical thought has never motivated anyone to do anything. The 'small reason', as he called this above, has always left me indifferent and can thus at best be used for projects of bad faith; that is, for pretending that my actions were the results of proper logical thinking.

But what does Nietzsche then mean to argue when saying that 'if this thought gained possession of you, it would change you as you are or perhaps crush you. The question in each and every thing, "Do you desire this once more and innumerable times more?" would lie upon your actions as the greatest weight' (GS 274)? Now, with respect to Kant we have seen that the moral law cannot ground itself on merely practical considerations, as it would then have to find its motivation in self-will, which is to say, in something essentially immoral. The voice of the demon is thus no longer a moral voice in the proper sense of the word. And, indeed, in this formulation of the imperative, there is no reference to other human beings and hence no moral dimension in the sense that we generally understand it. This formulation of the law would hence already have located human action in a realm 'beyond good and evil'.

On the other hand, this reformulation brings out the vacuous nature of the categorical imperative, thereby following a critique on the part of Friedrich Wilhelm Joseph Schelling (1775–1854), a contemporary and friend of Hegel. Schelling rephrases the problem that Kant had already seen with respect to the incompatibility of the knowledge we have of the world and our moral freedom, insofar as he offers the criticism that with respect to the moral law, we are either already good in order then to listen to its command, or we are evil, in which case we will not hear it. Consequently, one cannot see how the law should motivate the being-evil of someone to become being-good. Nietzsche thus does not evaluate the 'success' of this thought with respect to making a decision concerning this or that action, based on the further premise that 'I could have done otherwise', but turns it towards the affirmation of myself, which is to say, as a thought motivating myself to 'become the one that I am'. Here I do not represent myself as a doer behind a deed which I could on principle separate from my self, but I affirm or deny all of my actions insofar as these make me the one who I am. We could here return to Leibniz' example of Judas, which was discussed in the first chapter above. Here the question was not 'Why have I done what I have done?', but 'Can I take responsibility for the self that has done this act?'

The notion of moral responsibility does not attach itself to an act of rational deliberation which sees a particular action grounded on a reasonable choice, but, insofar as this infinite action grounds my own being, I here choose myself. This thought thus distinguishes not between this or that logically possible act, but, first of all, between the authentic affirmation of my being and the inauthentic despair of a life that cannot affirm itself. The ethical version of *Eternal Recurrence* hence concerns the affirmation of my own existence. It gives the 'highest confirmation and seal' to the 'who' that I am. Having seen above that the aim of philosophy is to demonstrate the identity of freedom and necessity in the affirmation of my being, we can see here that the ethical version of the *Eternal Return of the Same* does precisely this, namely grounding the notion of my freedom not on the level of knowledge as opposed to the 'outside' world, but on the level of my being inseparable from the world of action.

The question is thus how I respond to the thought, which is to say, whether I merely think it and come to the conclusion that thought itself is incapable of making a difference in the world, or whether the thought 'takes possession' of me, leading to an affirmation of my existence. This 'either/or' might remind us of Leibniz when he compared materialism with idealism, saying that these two imply specific hierarchies between entities. Materialism, in the final analysis, builds up the hierarchy of beings on its interpretation of matter, which is to say, according to the principle of passivity, while Idealism bases all beings on the notion of the idea, of God or mind, thereby looking at the world from the perspective of freedom. As Leibniz added, there is no argument or evidence that could arbitrate between the two, that could show one as true and the other as false, so that, in the end, we are free to choose the more advantageous interpretation. Nietzsche agrees that the decision is not one based on good reasons which I might give for one or the other interpretation, but he furthermore argues that it is not a question of an ungrounded choice either. The interpretation of the thought in one direction or the other is an expression of my own being, in which I show myself as being either 'weak' or 'strong'. The thought does not make a decision between different classes of actions, but between different kinds of acting beings.

This is how the thought of the *Eternal Return of the Same* is supposed to become a historical crisis of humankind, as it sorts the strong from the weak, the ones able to surmount nihilism from those who will perish from it. This is the reason why Nietzsche calls himself, the thinker of *Eternal Recurrence*, a 'dynamite' and 'destiny', as this thought will cut history asunder. The crisis hence is at once historical, in that it marks the end of the metaphysical understanding of the human being as the halfway house between heaven and earth, thereby finding the meaning of our contemporary, nihilistic age in the *Overhuman*, and practical, in that it divides the weak from the strong, which is to say, the passive suffering of nihilism from an active nihilism of strength. For us who think this thought, the decision is therefore not that of 'becoming' animal or *Overhuman*, but remaining in the state of the passive nihilism of the last men or of realizing the illness and turning to the active nihilism of the higher men. The step from passive nihilism to active nihilism is thus the step from a passive representation of the problem in a logical form to the active experience of *Eternal Recurrence*.

iii. THE EXPERIENCE OF THE *ETERNAL RETURN OF THE SAME*

We have found two interpretations of the *Eternal Return of the Same*, the cosmological or ontological, on the one hand, and the ethical, on the other. Both seem to be quite straightforward, sometimes downright banal. And yet they can take on this impression of banality precisely because they crystallize the essence of our own existence. That is, they appear to us banal because their meaning seems to be self-evident. We are these halfway houses between heaven and earth and, having arrived at the end of the Platonic age, these two sides of our being have come unstuck. One interpretation sees the world as pure necessity; the other tries to grasp our freedom.

The task is then to bring these together, and this task has already been approached in that it is here the same thought, the same teaching, which gives expression to both freedom and necessity. And yet these two seem to be opposed to each other and therefore we cannot hope to 'mend' them back together again in some conservative fashion. That is to say, many people nowadays claim that we should mend the ills of contemporary society by finding a way back to the old values which have made life and order possible in the past. And yet, as Nietzsche says, *God is Dead* and God remains dead; no intentional act of the human being will bring him back to life. In other words, the human being as this halfway house between heaven and earth, between mind and body, is coming to an end. And the thought of the *Eternal Return of the Same* is a means to bring it to this end. But what is this end? What comes after it? Early on Zarathustra makes this quite clear: 'The human being is a rope, fastened between animal and *Overhuman*' (Z 4). Coming to the end of the rope, the human being takes on the form of what Nietzsche calls the *Last Man*. This last man is the contemporary humanist of the scientific age. He interprets himself as the end and purpose of creation and, hence, resists the historical movement that would carry him beyond himself. This resistance takes the form of reducing everything that is to the present: thus the world is a world of facts, and thoughts are present representations or beliefs. We still think of something like the future, but this is meant only to preserve the present, to leave space for those who we are. The Last Man thus 'questions and questions and never tires: "How may man preserve himself best, longest, most agreeably?" With that – [these Last Men] are the masters of the present' (Z 298). Insofar as the human being is this master of the present and insofar as this mastery is called metaphysics, philosophers have spoken since the middle of the twentieth century of a 'Metaphysics of Presence'.

But, as Nietzsche argues, the human being lives historically and the only truth that allows it to live is historically grounded. The Last Man hence suffers, without knowing, from the historical malady. Therefore the thought of the *Eternal Return of the Same* necessarily starts out from this illness, insofar as it is addressed to us. It takes the position of an extra-historical view not because it believes in the justification of such a view, but because this is the view that determines modernity. In the thought of the *Eternal Return of the Same* this idea of time as infinity is itself put into question, insofar as it is shown to be contradictory. Instead of now turning against the thought of the *Eternal Return of the Same*, to denounce it as the truth of the contemporary human being, the thought of *Eternal Recurrence* has itself to be understood in its temporal sense, which is here to say, in the change that it undergoes

145

while taking possession of the thinker. We could make this point clearer in the following way: what would be the sense of criticizing the modernity of the last men if this critique were not able to carry us forwards in its very terms? If there were a difference between the critique and the solution, then we would have been returned to the powerlessness of the ideal.

To think, as Nietzsche had already said in the essay 'On Truth and Lying in a Non-Moral Sense', is itself an action, which is to say, is itself to be understood according to beginning, development and end. In other words, thought finds its fulfilment first in the experience of thinking. An experience is something that changes us as it happens to us, and it is for this reason that we have continuously said that a thought can be thought only in its movement. It picks us up somewhere and moves us somewhere else. The teacher of the *Eternal Recurrence* must hence, at the same time, be the teacher of the *Overhuman*.

Therefore we have to understand this experience as it is most clearly engaged in the *Zarathustra*. Only by grasping this experience can we have an insight into the reason why Nietzsche presents this thought not only as the greatest weight, but also as a riddle. Why should there be a riddle where we have found only two relatively banal ideas? Because the movement of thought itself cannot be represented clearly and distinctly, it cannot be dissolved into ideas and hence, in the *Zarathustra*, takes recourse to allegory. The *Zarathustra*, the 'deepest book ever bequeathed to mankind', is thus the deepest, if only because it is not flat, because the truth cannot be given clearly and distinctly, but only against the background of the depth of historical time.

Nietzsche explores the experience of the thought of *Eternal Recurrence* most explicitly in the chapter 'Of the Vision and the Riddle' at the beginning of the third book of the *Zarathustra* (Z 176–180). We have spoken of the two faces of the thought and, indeed, the German title of the chapter, literally translated, is 'Of the Face and the Riddle'. Insofar as this riddle concerns the experience of the thought, which is to say, goes beyond the representation of the two faces – the ontological and the ethical interpretation – it is no longer presented to the last man. To understand this experience one has already to have had an insight into the significance of the death of God, insofar as this concerns the abolition of the true and the apparent world. Or, while the formulation of the two faces concerned the situation of the human being expressed in Kantian transcendental philosophy, clearly separating that which can be known from that which cannot be known, Zarathustra presents the thought to those who have left Kantianism behind.

In the *Critique of Pure Reason*, Kant gives an image of the task of his critical philosophy. Insofar as critique here means to establish the lawful limits of knowledge, he likens this to an island, which is to say, to the finite land where one has solid ground under one's feet. This island of reason is surrounded by the wild sea as the realm to which our desires often entice us, but where there is no secure knowledge to be gained. The madman of section 125 of *The Gay Science* had already declared the end of this island of reason consequent to the death of God and here, in the *Zarathustra*, Nietzsche thus addresses the thought of the *Eternal Return of the Same* to 'bold venturers and adventurers and whoever has embarked with cunning sails upon dreadful seas', to those 'intoxicated by riddles' rather than by clear and distinct ideas, to those who 'take pleasures in twilight' and have therefore left the Enlightenment ideals behind them, and thus, too, to those who have given up on calculative thought, to those who 'hate to calculate' where they can guess (Z 176). The experience of the thought is thus open only to those who have understood the nihilistic essence of modernity, who have understood the historical malady and are now seeking a cure. These addressees of the riddle will later be called the 'higher men'. To these alone *Zarathustra* addresses the riddle. And this riddle he calls the vision of 'the face of the most solitary man'.

The riddle begins with Zarathustra climbing up a mountain path, which, as we will see shortly, signifies the experience of the thought as it carried him above the market square of the Last Men. But ascending this mountain is an arduous task, the more so as Zarathustra is, at the same time, pulled downwards by the *Spirit of Gravity*, whom he calls 'his devil and arch-enemy' (Z 177). Who is this *Spirit of Gravity*? As always with philosophical determinations, we have to be careful. The *of* in this name will not distinguish one *Spirit* from all the others, but it will provide an essential definition of that which is *Spirit*. Now *Spirit* here translates the German *Geist*, often also translated as *Mind*. Having considered, in the first chapter, Nietzsche's redefinition of the mind–body problem as the strife between the 'small reason' and the 'great reason', between consciousness and embodied thought, and realizing that the *Spirit of Gravity* sits on his shoulders, it is not too difficult to see that it is this strife that is here dramatised. Zarathustra tries to surmount the essence of the human being as the hybrid of mind and body, but the mind resists and tries to pull him down. It does so on account of its restriction to formal logic – that is, the *Spirit of Gravity* objects to Zarathustra that everything that goes up has to go down again, that a stone thrown up has to fall down again. In other words, he tells Zarathustra that the whole endeavour of surmounting himself is doomed to fail from the outset. This spirit sits upon him, 'half dwarf, half mole; crippled, crippling; pouring lead-drops into my ear, leaden thoughts into my brain' (Z 177).

'I ascended, I dreamt, I thought, – but All depressed me' (Z 177): while the first activities are for Nietzsche activities ascribed to the body, the All is a product of mind, and, indeed, its most proper product. It is, first of all, the logical universality of thought conceived of in Plato, which thinks everything with respect to a universal form: the All. It is in the face of this All that the human being is stifled. And spirit is the *Spirit of Gravity* precisely because it lays the weight of the All on the shoulders of the human being, which it can only do by way of representation, so that what has no resemblance can still be aligned, categorized, archived in one single consciousness. The contradiction, in the literal sense, of 'small' and 'great' reason is thus quite strange. While the latter is more encompassing than the former, the 'small reason' embraces the universal, that is, the All, precisely insofar as it reduces its object to the present. And this present is something one cannot escape: in the medium of this All, all movement is impossible. That is why we have found in the *Antichrist* the characterization of the last men, as those who are everything, everything that knows not where to turn. For these last men, thought cannot be anything other than objective representation of abstract logical relations, but as such it always already appears as superfluous, impotent. The *Spirit of Gravity* is thus Zarathustra's most intimate enemy, belonging to the history of his own thought, condemning him to the solitude of an alienation of body and mind into two: 'So as a couple, one is truly more lonely than on one's own' (Z 177).

Insofar as the *Spirit of Gravity* is discouraging Zarathustra, the latter responds with courage, thereby showing that the thought of the 'great reason' does not shut out the emotive basis of thinking. Courage certainly is something belonging to thought, to the path of thinking, but it cannot be dissolved into logical results. To think with or without courage thus makes no difference to the 'small reason', but all the difference to Zarathustra. Often, on first reading the *Zarathustra*, one might be tempted to ignore much of the 'stylistic' form and think that many a remark belongs, so to speak, to the 'story' more than to the philosophical argument. And yet, after a while the reader realizes that every word in the *Zarathustra* is placed with the utmost care of composition, that no word here appears by accident. Courage answers the question of why one thinks, and thus of the direction of thinking, thereby belonging to a long tradition of philosophy reflecting on the affective motivation of thought, which is to say, reflecting on the passions as the foundation of all human thought. But, first of all, Nietzsche here marks a difference between the 'small reason', encapsulated in the presence of logical representation, on the one hand, and the 'great reason', with its potentials of movement, development and change, on the other hand.

Consequently this courage makes Zarathustra stop and challenge the *Spirit of Gravity* with the riddle of the *Eternal Return of the Same* – that is, the riddle of time – a riddle, thus, which the dwarf cannot possibly understand, as his thought remains within the timeless presence of formal representation. Where they have stopped, there is a gateway:

'Look at this gateway, dwarf! . . . it has two aspects. Two paths come together here: no one has ever reached their end.

'This long lane behind us: it goes on for an eternity. And this long lane ahead of us – that is another eternity.

'They are in opposition to another, these paths; they abut on one another: and it is here at this gateway that they come together. The name of the gateway is written above it: "Moment".

'But if one were to follow them further and ever further and further: do you think, dwarf, that these paths would be in eternal opposition?' (Z 178)

The dwarf answers disdainfully. For him there is no riddle, as the solution to this problem is quite simple. Two straight paths which abut one another, while still leading to the same location, namely infinity, must make up a circle. 'Everything straight lies . . . time itself is a circle', he answers. Both are here answering the question

'What is time?' and do they not both give the same answer? Namely that time is a circle and repeats itself infinitely? Is this not what we have learned about the ontological version of *Eternal Recurrence*? But we have already seen, on the one hand, that an answer in the form of a sentence like 'this is that' has a meaning which refers back to the one who said it, insofar as it refers back to its emotive basis, and, on the other hand, that such objective representation places itself outside of time in order to look at time, which is itself impossible.

Having said that the question 'What is being?' is led back by Nietzsche to a typology, to the question 'Who says being?', the difference between the words of Zarathustra and the dwarf seems to be rather imperceptible. Both characterize time as a circle, and yet the distance between them is so immense that they immediately lose sight of each other. Both seem to say the same, but the same is each time said from a different perspective. But this is not to say that the difference is posed as a difference of authority. If we think of the thought of *Eternal Recurrence* here as a teaching, in order to understand the motion of thought, then we can see that any one phrase always expresses the sense of the sentence preceding it, and therefore the sense of the assertion 'time is a circle' depends on the voice that has pronounced it, or, rather, on the sentences that form its history. This is precisely the infinite regress of sense which was supposed to be stopped by representational thought. While the latter merely expresses a logical entity, Zarathustra makes it clear that these logical entities themselves belong to the flow of time:

> 'And this slow spider that creeps along in the moonlight, and this moonlight itself, and I and you at this gateway whispering together, whispering of eternal things – must we not all have been here before?' (Z 179)

The *Eternal Return of the Same* has thus made the point that time is itself historical, that our understanding of time as clock time belongs to our misunderstanding of truth as eternal truth, and that we have consequently to understand not only what the *Eternal Return of the Same* says about historical existence, but also in what sense the thought of the *Eternal Return of the Same* is itself historical. This is to say that rather than being indifferent to the actual historical moment that it describes, *it is concrete in that it understands its own appearance as specifying its content.* Everything returns, as the *Eternal Return of the Same* stipulates, even this thought of the *Eternal Return of the Same* itself.

We have seen, in Chapter 2, that Nietzsche distinguishes between the historical and the traditional notion of truth as correctness of representation, which he has demonstrated in 'On Truth and Lying in a Non-Moral Sense' as metaphorical in its essence. Such truth is untruth in that it is not capable of speaking about the world. This is why, in the *Antichrist*, he says that Jesus Christ speaks only in metaphors. That is to say, while he appears to speak of this world, the meaning of his speech is pointing to the world beyond: he speaks not of this life, but of the afterlife. The same holds for conceptual language generally: here one appears to speak about the finite world in which we live, while really referring to universal conceptions quite indifferent to this world. It was for the same reason that Nietzsche claims, as we saw in Chapter 3, that in the mathematical sciences 'reality does not even appear as a problem'.

Here, equally, the *Spirit of Gravity* uses the image of the circle as a metaphor for time, while Zarathustra is drawn into the allegory or simile (*Gleichnis*) of *Eternal Recurrence*. As a metaphor this thought leaves the *Spirit of Gravity* indifferent, while it has taken possession of Zarathustra and has, thus, moved him. It has changed Zarathustra, and is itself changing. This is why the *Spirit of Gravity* vanishes from Zarathustra's sight. A few lines later Zarathustra thus wonders: 'Where had the dwarf now gone? And the gateway? And the spider? And the whispering?' (Z 179)

The dwarf cannot understand that the thought of the *Eternal Return of the Same* determines itself in its historical appearance as an answer to nihilism. He cannot understand that this nihilism appears by means of the abolition of concrete time for the sake of the eternal Now, and it is precisely for this reason that he disappears from Zarathustra's vision. The *Spirit of Gravity* no longer inhabits the same questions as Zarathustra, and it was indeed the whole task of this episode to show that the dwarf had no right to rise upwards, to show that he could only have risen upwards on Zarathustra's shoulders, and, *consequently*, that Zarathustra had a right to rid himself of him. The riddle of the *Eternal Return of the Same* thus addresses itself only to Zarathustra, the thinker of the 'great reason' of the body, who now comes to see it as 'the face of the most solitary man'. This refers to the image of a young shepherd now coming into view, suffocated by a black snake that has crawled into his mouth. It is not too difficult to see this as an image of man suffering the thought of *Eternal Recurrence*. Zarathustra tells of his attempts to pull the snake out of his mouth, to help him to get rid of his suffering, and yet it is only with courage, rather than good argument, that the shepherd can bite its head off and spit it out.

Certainly, this allegory does not provide us with much understanding concerning the question of the overcoming of nihilism. All it illustrates is the process of the realization of the illness of nihilism and the impossibility of overcoming such nihilism by means of good ideas, therefore adding that the 'rationality' of the 'small reason' is not of much help here. As a riddle which resists calculation, it is the riddle of the coming into being of the *Overhuman*. And yet, as we will see in the last section of this chapter, this coming into being of the *Overhuman* will for us always remain a riddle, which is to say, the object of a desire that cannot be fulfilled in our presence.

Is this all that the *Zarathustra* can tell us about the experience of the *Eternal Return of the Same*? Eleven sections later, in 'The Convalescent', Zarathustra again calls on his thought. As we have seen again and again, this does not mean that he applies more logical skills to develop it further, but he speaks of the thought taking possession of him. If we have understood the body, the 'great reason', mostly as something passive, here too thought is experienced as an affect, as the task of the incorporation of our greatest errors. Having called on his thought, Zarathustra falls unconscious, wakes up, and neither talks nor leaves his cavern for seven days. At the end of these seven days the world returns to him and his animals decide that it is now time to talk to him. While his animals now enter into a long and often poetic discourse on the *Eternal Recurrence* of all natural things, Zarathustra remains mostly silent, and, if he speaks at all, this is to liken the animals' discourse to that of man and his cruelties. This discourse on *Eternal Recurrence* is thus not Zarathustra's either. Considering that, as Nietzsche says in his notebooks from the time when he was writing the *Zarathustra*, it is the consequence of Zarathustra that the human being, in order not to suffer from this thought, has to develop back to animal life or forwards towards the *Overhuman* (10/479F), here we encounter merely the discourse of the animals. To understand more of the thought of the *Eternal Return of the Same*, we thus have to follow the clue that the teacher of the *Eternal Return of the Same* is also the teacher of the *Overhuman*.

iv.   LAST HUMAN, HIGHER HUMAN AND OVERHUMAN

We have created the most difficult thought – now let us create the creature for which it is light and beatific.

1883

The notion of the *Übermensch* in Nietzsche's works has long attracted considerable interest and it is perhaps not too surprising that much of this interest has led to sometimes amusing and some-times catastrophic interpretations. Thus in particular the National Socialists of the German Third Reich have made out of this *Über-mensch* the caricature of a self-willed 'Blond Beast'. The first trans-lation of this term in Nietzsche's texts as the '*Superman*' has only worsened this absurd image. This idea of the *Superman* 'having' a great *Will to Power* by means of which he would subjugate other humans has, unfortunately, held sway for a long time. This is not on account of any close reading of his works, but simply because that is how one could easily understand the terms *Will to Power* and *Superman*. Consequently, many translators have adopted the more literal translation '*Overman*'. This translation makes more sense in terms of the *Über*, but still suffers from implying a single individual. But Nietzsche does not speak about an individual male or female human being, but about the historical existence of the 'human being'. Therefore, although it is grammatically more cumbersome, I have in these pages decided to adhere to the literal translation of the word *Übermensch* as '*Overhuman*'.

The age of the human being as the halfway house between heaven and earth comes to an end in the suffering of nihilism. As, after the *Death of God*, history appears as infinitely open, this human being appears in the pre-historical sequence of all kinds of animals. After Darwin, this human being has realized that it has not been conceived by the gods, but that it, like any other animal, has a rather low origin. Instead of calling God its father, it has found the ape at its origins. To speak of the human being as the rope tied between animal and *Overhuman* is hence, first of all, to see the historical finitude of the human as well as of any living being.

But why is the life-form following the human being still called Over-*human*? Because the future is something which is not given to us as a clear and distinct idea. In an absurd thought experiment, we could look at this from the point of view of the ape: what if the ape had been able to consider the future and to realize that in this future it would come to an end? Insofar as it would not have known what the future brings, indeed insofar as the future as future is in principle unknowable, it would have only been able to call it that which will follow its own being. As such it might have called it the *Overape*. Only once this future had become a reality would this *Overape* turn out to be the human being, while from the perspective of the ape this point would have remained without significance. Nietzsche similarly speaks of the future of the human being as the *Overhuman*.

In opposition to such careful and limited representation, we often want to understand what this *Overhuman* 'is', by affixing predicates to this word. And yet, affixing attributes to a thing means to determine it in its presence, while the *Overhuman* is precisely not yet present. You can see here again the Nietzschean critique of time. We tend to understand the different temporal stages of past, present and future by reducing them to presence-gone, presence-present and presence-to-be, so that we can understand those entities not belonging to our presence equally as present things. The same holds for the idea of utopia, where one paints the idea of a present lying in the future. But Nietzsche has already shown that this idea of a universality of representation belongs to the misrepresentation of time, to those sensations of space and time that lead us into error. To see that the teacher of the *Overhuman* is equally the teacher of *Eternal Recurrence* is thus to understand that the future cannot be thought of by us as a presence to come. Sure, if we look at the position of the ape in our example, we can say that the presence of the human being was its future, but that again would remain an abstract representation. If the future had any significance for the presence of the ape, this future would precisely not have been the presence of the human being.

'Behold, I teach you the Overman' thus means at the same time 'I teach you the inhuman', in the sense of teaching that which is no longer human. As Nietzsche says, the Overhuman will relate to

Man like Man today relates to the ape – by way of negation. The Overhuman will say – emphatically – *I am not a human being, a human being is this unfitting hybrid, this being that by way of its constitution has already been determined as weakness.* This thought of the *Overhuman* thus presupposes the critique of time, stipulating that past, present and future can no longer be levelled into presence-gone, presence-present and presence-to-be – and that in turn means that the 'Overhuman' is not simply the man who will live in a century's time. This is the whole problem in considering the *Overhuman*, in other words: the ontological status of past, present and future 'things' differs.

Someone who can see the future in the form of a present image we call not a philosopher but a prophet. Such a prophet has his eyes no longer on this world, but on the future as another world which will come to pass. The philosopher, on the other hand, is fully immersed in this world; he tries to see the world, so to speak, from the inside and, therefore, there is but one world for him. Nietzsche clarifies this point in the *Genealogy of Morality*. Having exalted the idea of the *Overhuman* in a rather enthusiastic passage, ending with the line '*he must come one day*' (GM 71), Nietzsche immediately checks himself and concludes: '– But what am I saying? Enough! Enough! At this point just one thing is proper, silence'. Nietzsche is generally not very positive concerning prophecy, and where he does seem to be, he demonstrates that what appears as prophecy to us is spoken from the position of a finer and more sensitive experience, in the same way as when we grant frogs the ability to prophesy the weather.

Thus insofar as Nietzsche has anything to say about the *Overhuman*, this is generally 'negative', i.e. derived from the suffering that gives rise to our longing for the *Overhuman*: that he will stand to the human being as the human being stands to the ape; that the thought of *Eternal Recurrence* will be easy for him to bear; that he will no longer be this hybrid of ghost and plant; that we might imagine him as Julius Caesar with the heart of Jesus Christ, etc., but none of these remarks could count as an attribute of a present being. Therefore, neither Nietzsche nor Zarathustra ever says anything like 'become the *Overhuman*' or 'serve the *Overhuman*', but 'let the *Overhuman* be the meaning of this earth', while a present human being cannot *be* a meaning at all.

You will often find section three of the *Antichrist* cited as a proof that Nietzsche did not think of the *Overhuman* as that which follows the human being. Here Nietzsche says: 'The problem I raise here is not what ought to succeed mankind in the sequence of species . . .: but what type of human being one ought to *breed*, ought to *will*, as more valuable, more worthy of life, more certain of the future' (AC 126). But does this really contradict to what we have been saying here? If it did, we would find a fundamental contradiction in Nietzsche's work, putting into question not only the idea of the *Overhuman*, but also the historical nature of the thought of *Eternal Recurrence* and the notion of the *Will to Power*. And yet, as we will see, there is no contradiction here. The human being is indeed an end and is at an end, and the history of humanity is not seen by Nietzsche in the form of a progress that leads to the *Overhuman* as a still higher crown of creation. Indeed, it is not up to the human being to 'produce' the *Overhuman* or to make itself the *Overhuman*.

While, speaking in the abstract, we might come to see the human being as a tightrope between animal and *Overhuman*, concretely speaking, that is to say, from the perspective of the human being, what is given is its end. This end it experiences as nihilism and the thought of the *Eternal Return of the Same* was supposed to make a difference. But this difference for us is first of all that between passive nihilism and active nihilism, whereby the former is understood as its repression and the latter as its realization. This difference Nietzsche expresses in the difference between the Last Men and the Higher Men. Insofar as this difference is to become meaningful by means of the thought of the *Overhuman* as the meaning of this earth, it must be possible to characterize it with respect to their respective stances towards the future. We have already seen this point with respect to the Last Men. These understand themselves as the high point of creation, as beings of an absolute value, for whom there is, consequently, nothing to do. The Last Men can see the future only as the preservation of their own presence: with this they are masters of the present. Thinking about the *Overhuman* can mean for them nothing other than to think about their own possibilities. They might thus embrace the idea as one of self-empowerment, as a possible justification of their private egoism, and their empty feeling of superiority. This is empty, as Nietzsche argued, because the world no longer offers them anything of worth. The masters of the present are thus the ones without future and they are, as such, tired of the world in that they are unable to see in it anything but themselves. And even beyond their death they still see themselves as determining the 'fatherland' of their offspring. Nowadays, as they have given up on the idea of eternal life in heaven, they even think they might cheat death completely by inventing some genetic cure for this presumed 'illness'. Zarathustra judges these Last Men to be 'the *most harmful species of man*, because they preserve their existence as much at the expense of *truth* as at the expense of the *future*' (EH 99).

And yet, as Nietzsche says, those who still have a future are not looking for their mastery over this future in terms of determining such a 'fatherland' by perennializing their own presence. Instead creation for them means to create something beyond themselves, namely to make way for the land of their children, which Nietzsche called the 'Childland'. Here our instinctive response to the notions of 'strength' and 'weakness' seems to be perverted, in that those who master the future are called 'weak', while the 'strong' are those of whom Zarathustra says that 'they desire their own downfall'. We will see again with the notion of the *Will to Power* that this is not a coincidence or contradiction, but that Nietzsche tries to teach us a lesson concerning these ideas of what is weak and what is strong. Insofar as he argued in the *Genealogy of Morality* that our contemporary morality concerns an inversion of the values of 'good' and 'evil' and of 'weak' and 'strong', we should expect our instincts to judge these quite wrongly. From here follows the grotesque interpretation of the 'Superman' as the one who, without any regard for others and the world at large, would merely affirm his private egoisms by 'doing others in'. This interpretation is thus derived from the vantage point of slave-morality, dreaming of a release from its impotence in the face of the world, and the resentful idea of freedom as a 'freedom from . . . others', behind which hides a tiredness of life and a tiredness of the world; in short, passive nihilism.

We can see here again the difference between the 'great reason' and the 'small reason': freedom as attributed to the abstract, concentrated mind is always a 'freedom from', insofar as the mind itself is conceived of in abstraction from the world. Its ideal is thus to abstract itself from the world, to demonstrate its independence. As soon as, on the other hand, freedom is attributed to the body, to the 'great reason', its ideal points in the opposite direction, namely towards that which it can do, towards the degree that it can do things in the world, and that is also to say, to the degree that it can integrate itself in its world. This freedom Nietzsche calls a 'freedom to . . .', expressing itself as a faithfulness towards the world. 'Free from what? Zarathustra does not care about that! But your eye should clearly tell me: free *for* what?' (Z 89). The Last Men are those who cannot create anything beyond their own endurance, their mastery over the present. Yet insofar as the problem of history is the problem of creation, they are bringing history to a close.

Here, history is in need of the teaching of *Eternal Recurrence*, is in need 'of a doctrine, strong enough to have a formative effect: strengthening the strong, crippling and destructive for those tired of the world' (11/69). But these 'strong' ones are not on the cusp of becoming *Supermen*, they are the *Higher Men*, for whom the *Over-human* is the meaning of this earth. These *Higher Humans* are active nihilists. They realize that human existence in our age is coming to a crisis and that this crisis cannot just be explained away. And yet, they see this crisis as a historical rather than a personal transition from human being to *Overhuman*. The whole fourth book of the *Zarathustra* is dedicated to understanding these Higher Humans. Insofar as Nietzsche is here describing in similes the founding of a new age, he does so in the imagery of the last founding of a new age, that is, in Christian terms. Zarathustra returns to his cave in the mountains. He describes himself as the fisher, who has caught men with his deepest thought. On his way he comes across one after another of these Higher Men, who have all been seeking him in order to become his disciples. These Higher Men are representatives from all walks of life, from religion and science, from politics and from the arts, from myth and philosophy, from the literati and the public. They all come together for the Last Supper in order, then, to disperse again.

That these Higher Men are nihilists becomes clear immediately from their description and their actions. They are searching for a teacher, because they have lost their direction and their faith. They attempt to dissimulate themselves and to appear less needy than they are. If they are the 'last pope' or the 'scientist', they realize that their position is untenable and often quite ridiculous. They have thus lost the pride of the last men and this is precisely their virtue. While passive nihilism consisted in the unwillingness to concede that one lives one's life without any aims, the Higher Men often appear pathetic in their avowed aimlessness. They are ashamed of what they are and of what little they know or can do. These Higher Men seem confused, but they are confused because the world has taken hold of them. As Nietzsche said in *The Gay Science*, 'what distinguishes the higher human beings from the lower is that the former see and hear immeasurably more, and see and hear thoughtfully' (GS 241).

The creative power that Nietzsche outlines here is both affective and, in an essential sense, creating beyond oneself. It is for this reason that the Higher Men give rise to hope, to the very degree that their future is open and that this openness implies their modesty. One should never underestimate the rigour in Nietzsche's use of words. Thus everyone agrees that the path to the *Overhuman* has to take the form of a self-overcoming, while one often forgets that it is precisely this self which is to be overcome in this creative act. When Zarathustra speaks of his love towards these Higher Men, he thus links this love to the will to one's own end: 'I love him who wants to create beyond himself, and thus perishes' (Z 91). Neither Zarathustra nor these Higher Men are or claim to be *Overhumans* – indeed, 'we' humans are never to be '*Overhumans*' – but they lay claim to understand the *Overhuman* as the meaning of their existence, thereby understanding themselves to be the 'sowers of the future' (4/246).

v. THE *ETERNAL RETURN OF THE SAME* AS RELIGION

In our consideration of the early essay *On the Advantages and Disadvantages of History for Life*, we have seen that Nietzsche understands the essential task of historical creation as the self-creation of humankind. Here it was a question of giving oneself a second nature as that nature which one would have wanted to have. Such a second nature is brittle and precarious and might often seem unwarranted with respect to the first, which has the persuasion of the tradition and of habit, of feeling and instincts behind it. And yet, there again, what gave hope to this second nature is the realization that what we call our first nature was once itself such a second nature, i.e. was itself the result of a historical creation. The courage for such creation thus thrives on the realization that there is no fact with regard to human nature, that creation is possible, and it is this insight, furnished by the thought of the *Eternal Return of the Same*, which lies behind the stylistic repetition of the similes of the

Christian community and its 'Last Supper' by Zarathustra and his disciples. Our first nature is the Platonico-Christian idea of the human being as the halfway house between heaven and earth. The second nature here envisaged is first that of the 'free spirit', who has freed himself from this tradition and is free towards his own self-overcoming. We have also seen that any creation presupposes a destruction of historical value, so that these 'free spirits' are quite aware of their own finitude, aware of the fact that their value does not lie in themselves but in what they do with respect to the future.

Now it is quite clear from the idea of the body as the locus of thinking, from the notion of history as the sole content of philosophy, as well as from the temporal separation between the Higher Men and the *Overhuman*, that we are not here dealing with any 'individual' idea of self-overcoming. Insofar as I find myself originally in a historical society, insofar as I understand my will and instincts as bequeathed to me by history, Nietzsche said that the aim of philosophy as the breeding of a future being is 'political', and that it is only with his philosophy that we again discover the meaning of a 'great politics'. That is to say, this breeding is necessarily one that involves the whole community and that thus directs itself towards its communion. And yet questions concerning the communion of human beings, unless they are seen as logical entities, are religious questions. The word 'religion' in its twofold root from *relegere* (to pick up, to take into account) and *religare* (to connect, to fasten) essentially concerns that which keeps human beings together. And as they only are insofar as they are kept together, there has never been any society on this earth, any human being, without being bound by religion.

The thought of the *Eternal Return of the Same* thus also appears as a religious question. It does not, as the insight following from the *Death of God*, address itself directly to our modern scientific world-picture, insofar as this does not constitute something new within European history. For Nietzsche it does not even make sense to speak of science as 'the new religion', even though many public scientists today behave with a fervour that was once only found in a Sunday sermon. There were two things about science that we found out above: that it is 'art which has forgotten that it is art', which is to say that the sciences do not understand themselves and are thus not the right locus to seek such understanding; and that the sciences can be thought of as 'the shadow of the dead God', which is to say that they are essentially derivative from their Christian heritage.

In other words, there is a certain homology between the problem of nihilism following the death of God, on the one hand, and the various arguments for the existence of God, most notably by Plato and St Anselm, on the other, namely that they argue that without faith, the human being loses touch with the world. But what about Nietzsche? Is he not an atheist? We have often seen the contrast that Nietzsche reflects upon, between the Greek age of art and the modern age of science. In terms of religion, this is the contrast between our modern monotheistic Christian world and a poly-theistic society in which gods appear and disappear, in which Zeus is eaten by his father and freed again, in which Dionysos, a late immigrant from Asia, can still become the most revered god, as is professed even by Plato. These gods are representatives of a creative power, turning the whole of life into a question of art.

Our age, on the other hand, is, as Nietzsche says, characterized by 'two millennia, nearly, and not a single new God' (6/185). The teaching of the *Eternal Return of the Same* is supposed to bring European history to a crisis in which the strong are sorted from the weak. Strength and weakness have been seen to stand in relation to the concretion of life, and therefore as a furthering of life or a being tired of life. Hence the ability to believe in the thought is supposed to make a difference:

> This doctrine [of the *Eternal Return of the Same*] is merciful against those who do not believe in it, it does not contain any hells or other threats. Who does not believe has a *fleeting* life in his consciousness. (9/503)

It is not difficult to see the similarity of this statement to St Anselm's claim that the atheist is an idiot, as this again is somebody who might be highly intelligent, yet still 'has a fleeting life in his consciousness'. Our knowledge of the world has become unstuck from our desires, necessity from freedom, the body from the soul. Consequently, as we have just seen, thought appears to us as some-thing inessential and ephemeral, simply without consequence. Against this 'fleeting life' desire desires eternity. We have seen this in the roundelay, discussed in the introduction: 'all joy wants eternity, – Wants deep, deep, deep eternity', as the ultimate confirmation and seal of one's own, finite existence. The will is threatened with the loss of itself in the open horizon of history, in which everything barely seems to appear before it again disappears. Truth is, in all eternity, chaos. This idea of a 'fleeting life in one's consciousness' thus captures our understanding of animal life as one that has no world insofar as it cannot gain a foothold in existence. To find such a foothold has meant, since Plato, to be able to share in the divine infinite and to be able to value one's finite existence from birth to death only on account of such 'sharing in'. The Higher Men were then faced with valuing their existence as finite beings through their self-overcoming. To disappear meaningfully meant for the Higher Men to desire their own downfall for the sake of the future.

The thought of the *Eternal Return of the Same*, then, grounds a new conception of immortality – thereby changing the very idea of immortality itself. In this sense this thought constitutes a community of believers first of all as that of Zarathustra and his disciples. This is a community because it grants the possibility of communication through a renewed understanding of being, and they are believers insofar as the *Eternal Return of the Same* is a tautological ground that is made actual only through faith. A tautology is a circular argument, like, for example, the ontological argument, which says that only if you have faith in God can you understand the proof of God's existence. In a way similar to that in which the Christian God guaranteed both the identity of the community and the identity of the knower and the known by means of its own essence as that which is selfsame, the *Eternal Return of the Same* promises that once you believe in it, it is the circular ground of the identity of life. In other words, the *Eternal Return of the Same* is a tautology in a similar sense to the Christian God, and a tautology has to be believed in, otherwise it remains a stale logical contradiction and the image of death rather than of life. Furthermore, the thought of *Eternal Recurrence* is the original form of such tautology, insofar as it posits the circularity of existence.

The effectiveness of such a ground is thus not given logically, insofar as a tautological argument is, according to formal logic, a fallacy. Instead a tautology grounds itself historically, in the effective separation of past, present and future. The *Higher Men* exist in the open horizon of history, with their hope not attached to their own being, but to that which will follow their demise: 'Let us beware of teaching such a doctrine like a sudden religion! It has to sink in slowly, whole generations have to build on and become prolific through it . . .'

The best place to look for a summary of these different facets of the thought of the *Eternal Return of the Same* is the first note concerning what Nietzsche speaks of as a revelation that struck him during a walk in the Alps in August 1881 (9/494). This note is entitled 'The Return of the Same: Outline' and consists of five entries, itemizing the challenges posed to philosophical thought following the *Death of God*. The first entry speaks of 'the incorporation of the basic errors', which we have understood above as the realization that our own history has led to sensations of space and time, which have, in their turn, led us into the error of a reduction of the world to objective states of fact. It was from here that the teaching of the *Eternal Recurrence* took its starting point.

The second entry speaks of 'the incorporation of the passions'. We have seen that the 'error' of our history is to have led us into a contradiction between mind and body, between freedom and necessity. According to this error we have understood understanding itself as merely based on a logical level, as independent of the world and truth, as an adequation between sentences, as products of the mind, and things, as states of affairs. Descartes has thus understood the mind as a substance, which is to say, as something that cannot be directly touched by the world. But, as Nietzsche has argued, our instincts, our sensibility, our beliefs and even our thought are themselves passions, which is to say, we are in all our being affected by the historical world, and it is only on account of the incorporation of these passions that we can overcome the 'mind–body' problem.

The third entry qualifies this insight further, by speaking about knowledge as that which defines the human being: 'The incorporation of knowledge and of the knowledge that abstains (the passion of comprehension).' We can understand knowledge, as Nietzsche argues, as the highest affect. This is to say that we do not only understand thinking as a passion of discovering the world, but that thought itself is that which is given to us in our experience of life. But why would this knowledge be one that 'abstains'? Traditionally we have understood thought as the activity of the mind, an activity by means of which the human being was supposed to gain dominion over the world. Knowledge here simplifies and unifies the world. It uses categories which enforce an order onto that which in itself is chaotic. The understanding hence prescribes laws to nature, forcing it to obey where it commands. But what if thought was a part of the world? What if it could not distance itself from nature and understand itself as given separately from it? In other words, what if *God is Dead*? If these were so, then thought could no longer find its powers in its own laws, that is, in what we call rationality. These laws are, fundamentally, the law of non-contradiction, the law of sufficient reason and the law of the identity of indiscernibles. A knowledge that abstains from imposing its own limits onto the world would then have to suffer more truths, more different images of things. The question of truth would become for it one of strength, namely how much truth it could incorporate without perishing.

Here the thinker becomes herself an experiment with thought, an experiment trying to create that human being for whom the thought of the *Eternal Return of the Same* becomes something bearable and even something joyous. No longer responsible to a God, and being at the same time the experimenters and those experimented upon, these new thinkers are characterized by their innocence. The fourth entry reads: 'The innocent. The individual as experiment. The simplification of life, humiliation, attenuation – transition'. The *Higher Humans*, as we have seen, understand themselves as transitive, they are a passing-over and a going-under. In order to pass beyond the self-interpretation of the *Last Humans* as those of infinite worth, these *Higher Humans* are humiliated, their violence attenuated.

You might object that these *Higher Humans* are those of a higher *Will to Power*, and it is for this reason that we will now turn to that last, central notion in Nietzsche's work. But let us first see whether the last entry in the 'Outline' has by now become clear:

5   The new heavyweight: the Eternal Return of the Same. The infinite importance of our knowledge, our errors, of our habits and ways of life for all that comes. What are we to do with the rest of our life – we, who have spent the largest part of the same in essential ignorance? We teach the doctrine – this is the strongest means to incorporate it ourselves. Our type of happiness, as teachers of the most important doctrine. (9/494)

CONCLUSION: THE WILL TO POWER

The *Will to Power* is, next to the teaching of the *Eternal Return of the Same*, the most central thought in Nietzsche's philosophy. When Nietzsche says at the end of the 1880s that he can now see all his works coming together and wanting one thing, then this is given in the notion of *Will to Power*. While the *Will to Power* is a fundamental conception in Nietzsche's thought, while he uses it to understand this most ephemeral phenomenon that we call life, we can deal with it here in the form of a conclusion to our forays into Nietzsche's work, insofar as we have already encountered all the various developments of his thinking which make the notion of the *Will to Power* necessary.

We have found that Nietzsche understands philosophy and thinking generally in a sense quite different from the tradition. Thought, as being part of the world rather than as a disinterested gazing at the world, had to give up its theoretical absoluteness and thus, for example, the thought of *Eternal Recurrence* had to account for the fact that, like everything else, it arises in the world and disappears from it again, like a spider in the moonlight. In other words, there are no eternal truths and, consequently, no truths that hold always and for everyone. In short, Nietzsche is not a metaphysician who would provide a meta-theory concerning all of nature.

And yet the teaching of the *Eternal Return of the Same* seemed, first of all, to contradict this idea, when it appeared as a cosmological thesis. And what are we to do with the thought of the *Will to Power*, which Nietzsche describes in its most clear form thus: '*This world is the Will to Power – and nothing besides!* And you yourselves are this Will to Power – and nothing besides' (11/610; WP § 1067).

Can we imagine any sentence which sounds *more* metaphysical than this one? Metaphysics can be described as determining being as such and in general and doing so in the unity of the various philosophical disciplines, from ontology and ethics to politics and aesthetics. And this sentence concerning the *Will to Power* certainly seems to say that everything, all of being, you yourself and every human being is *Will to Power*. Not only every human being, but everything, from me to you, from bunny rabbits to brooks, from trees to stones, soil and air. And all these things are understood from the vantage point, not only of the will, but also of one particular will, namely that will which strives for power.

But let us be careful. We realized when we encountered arguments for the existence of God that these are all directed towards an understanding of the 'world' and that the world is in any case that which we experience and in which we experience ourselves. It is thus not making claims about an absolute, so to speak, an earth independent from such experience. We are thus not talking about any things-in-themselves or wondering about the question of whether everything would still be *Will to Power* even if there was no experience at all. To speak of the world here means not to look at it as if from outside, but to ask how it should be possible to look at it from within.

This world we often also call the 'life-world', and the notion of the *Will to Power* answers the claim that we have encountered above, namely to look at science from the perspective of art and at art from the perspective of life. We philosophers, being alive, try to understand the world in order to become active, in order to further life. What do we encounter in this world? To answer this question Nietzsche took a clue from science. We have seen in Leibniz the discovery of force and said that, insofar as we are looking at the world, insofar as we experience anything, this appears as a force. A force is not a thing that I can understand in isolation in order to see how it then interacts with others, but a force is always equal to its expression. It is only relation and nothing else. It is thus insofar as it is in the world. And it is in this respect that it is pure activity. Furthermore, when looking at Hegel, we have seen that the understanding, trying to understand the world, experiences itself as a force, which is to say as part of this world of forces.

But the natural sciences have made of this world of force something passive, factual, so that the understanding can get hold of it in terms of certain knowledge of the world. In this sense it has alienated the force of the understanding from the world. A force in science is something that can be numerically determined, and it is in this sense that it is not purely active. This is why Leibniz posited the principle of activity, so to speak, 'behind' the force and thereby in a metaphysical sense. But that means that life, the principle of self-movement, stands behind the world being divorced from its self-expression. It is for this reason that Nietzsche speaks of metaphysics as nihilism. Overcoming the separation between the true and the appearing world, abolishing both of them, means to collapse them into each other. The will is thus not the metaphysical truth of an appearing force, but the world is *Will to Power* and nothing besides.

To collapse these two worlds and their distinction is to posit the identity of freedom and necessity, of value and fact, of mind and body, as we have seen in our investigations into Nietzsche's thought. This can be done only from the perspective of art, insofar as art understands the notion of creation from out of the necessity of being. 'We must become the best learners and discoverers of everything that is lawful and necessary in the world: we must become *physicists* in order to be able to be *creators* . . .' (GS 266). This notion of creation thus no longer distinguishes between passive nature and the artistic qualities of a transcendent human being, but asserts that the human being can be free only insofar as it can find freedom within the world. Nietzsche thus argues that art is the clearest phenomenon of the *Will to Power* and that the world is 'a work of art giving birth to itself' (12/119).

Having announced the *Death of God* in section 108 of *The Gay Science*, Nietzsche asked himself how we might overcome the shadows of God. This question is synonymous with the question 'when may we begin to *naturalize* humanity in terms of a pure, newly discovered, newly redeemed nature?' (GS 169). The implications of this claim are now quite clear. As long as we look at the idea of nature in the modern sciences, we can certainly not naturalize the human being. In such nature there is no space for anything but a technologically fixed animal. This was why the teaching of the *Eternal Return of the Same* raised the decision of either animal or *Overhuman*. But looking at physics from the perspective of art, the *Will to Power* gives rise to the understanding of nature in terms of life. Conceived from this stance of the abolishment of the 'appearing world', nature is redeemed from its conception in the image of death.

We have seen that history has become the sole content of philosophy and that such a philosophy is also a philosophy of art, as art expresses the historical reality of the world. Now we can see that such a philosophy of art is also necessarily a philosophy of nature. It is for this reason that Nietzsche, in his notebooks from the 1880s, develops the beginnings of a physiology of art on the basis of the notion of the *Will to Power*. Art is here seen as expression of physiological processes, of an intoxication of the body, a hypersensitivity, or as arising from the imaginative world of dreams.

But what does this question of nature offer us here with respect to the understanding of the *Will to Power*? The *Will to Power* is an understanding of the world from the perspective of life. Too easily we understand this life from the perspective of consciousness. It is consciousness or at least the 'unconscious' which we understand to be the agent of willing. This consciousness *has* a will and it can arrest this will by knowing about it, by controlling it and by deliberating about its aims. From here follow most of the misunderstandings of Nietzsche's philosophy. The notion of a consciousness *having* a will allows us to understand the *Will to Power* only as a self-interested overpowering of everything that stands in its way. Consequently one links the notion of the *Will to Power* to violence and ignorance. Against this one sets the cultural control of these wild, natural instincts. We have seen already why this is not Nietzsche's understanding of the *Will to Power*.

The *Will to Power* cannot be understood as something that I, as a subject, *have* and which I can then exert or not exert in the world. To say that you are *Will to Power* and that the world is *Will to Power* is to break down the notion of subjectivity itself; that is, the distinction between subject and object as descriptions of experience. This is why the *Will to Power* undermines our ideas of subjective agency. These depend on the idea of responsibility by means of a strict separation between deliberation as a logical process and action in the world. Yet the *Will to Power* describes life as pure activity, unable to 'stop' itself and deliberate. This point, then, implies the whole of Nietzsche's critique of Christian morality.

The same point is at stake in the understanding of Nietzsche's perspectivism. This has often been taken to mean that any perspective that I might express in terms of an interpretation has its relative merits. But this is falling back into the vagaries and the voluntarism of 'beliefs' and 'views' which one might *have* of the world, and it is such a falling back because here we again silently presuppose that the 'I' that 'has' these perspectives is itself outside of all perspectives, so as to be able to 'choose' perspectives. And yet the notion of the *Will to Power* says that I *am* that perspective. This is thus not only a vague epistemological claim, but an ontological claim. True objectivity, Nietzsche claims, has nothing to do with the perspectiveless, which he argues is quite impossible, but with the plurality of perspectives.

We just have to recall that the will is understood according to the notion of force as something that exists only in relation to other forces. The will thus becomes the stronger, the more relations it can entertain. And if that is the case, then we can see that its activity is principally linked to an openness to affect, with an ability to be affected. The highest *Will to Power* – and we can see this with respect to the phenomenon of the artist – is thus that which can see more, hear more, experience more; which, in other words, can to a certain degree lose itself in the world, which is the least self-willed: 'There is *only* a perspectival seeing, *only* a perspectival "knowing"; and *the more* affects we allow to speak about a thing, *the more* eyes, different eyes, we know to make use of, the more complete will our "concept" of this thing, our "objectivity", be' (5/365). This affectivity was the reason why Nietzsche said in the first chapter that we philosophers are those 'who think and feel at the same time' (GS § 301).

To the question 'Who interprets?', Nietzsche answers: 'The *Will to Power*'. This interpretation leads to an understanding of oneself on living. Such understanding is in most cases not something I do know or even can know consciously. Darwin's finches interpret the world and thus understand themselves on living in various environments. Living, as Nietzsche says, is interpreting. All life is *Will to Power*.

Here we can see again Nietzsche's critique of Darwin's conception of evolution. According to this, the fundamental will is a will to self-preservation. Such a will would be a perverted will, in that it would will that nothing changes. It would restrict its will to the present, but that, as Nietzsche says, is absurd; it posits a fundamental passivity underlying the activity of interpretation. But since Plato's *Symposium* we know quite well that one cannot will what one has or just is. Willing itself is thus always a going beyond one-self, a creation into the future. This was the reason why Zarathustra said to the Higher Men: 'I love those who desire their own downfall' (Z 44); that is to say, those whose aim is not only to preserve themselves into their own future, who try to impose the fatherland onto all coming generations, but those who see life as self-overcoming. This is not the opposite of a will to self-preservation, it is not a desire for death, but an affirmation of life in the infinite horizon of becoming. We have found this above in terms of the *Overhuman*. Instead of advocating a self-willed desire to become the *Overhuman*, Zarathustra asked us to 'let the *Overhuman* be the meaning of this earth' (Z 42).

It has thus also become clear that the notion of the *Will to Power* is not intelligible in its distinction from other forms of the will. It does not stand in opposition to a will to kindness or a will to love, or whatever. From the perspective of life the will appears essentially as a *Will to Power*. To speak of an evolution of the human being as a being which cannot exist without truth thus means to derive the notions of will, freedom, knowing, consciousness, etc. from the idea of a redeemed nature, from life in the broader sense of the term.

But this might all sound a bit too benign. We just need to look at life and we realize that it is not exclusively a 'being nice to each other'. Certainly, life is overpowering; nature often appears as the question of 'eating or being eaten'; and human history, more so than any other, is a history of cruelty. Even education was seen as forcing the human being into a form. It was for this reason that Zarathustra, the teacher of *Eternal Recurrence*, had to be the advocate of suffering. And yet, as Nietzsche says, the idea of the *Eternal Recurrence* is, in opposition to Christian morality, the idea of 'sharing not suffering but joy' (GS 338).

FURTHER READING

READER

Ansell-Pearson, Keith & Duncan Large (eds), *The Nietzsche Reader* (Oxford: Blackwell, 2006).

INTRODUCTIONS

Ansell-Pearson, Keith, *How to Read Nietzsche* (London: Granta, 2005).
Copleston, Frederick, *A History of Philosophy*, Vol. 7, Part II, 'Schopenhauer to Nietzsche' (New York: Image Books, 1965).
Deleuze, Gilles, *Nietzsche and Philosophy* (London: Athlone, 1983).
Fink, Eugen, *Nietzsche's Philosophy*, (London: Continuum, 2003).
Hill, Kevin, *Nietzsche: A Guide for the Perplexed* (London: Continuum, 2007).
Vattimo, Gianni, *Nietzsche: An Introduction* (London: Continuum, 2001).

BIOGRAPHY

Safranski, Rüdiger, *Nietzsche: A Philosophical Biography* (London: Granta, 2003).

ESSAY COLLECTIONS

Allison, David B. (ed.), *The New Nietzsche* (Cambridge MA and London: MIT Press, 1977).
Lippitt, John and Jim Urpeth (eds), *Nietzsche and the Divine* (Manchester: Clinamen Press, 2000).
Magnus, Bernd and Kathleen M. Higgins (eds), *The Cambridge Companion to Nietzsche* (Cambridge: Cambridge University Press, 1996).
Sedgwick, Peter R. (ed.), *Nietzsche: A Critical Reader* (Oxford and Cambridge MA: Blackwell, 1995).

GENERAL TEXTS

Bataille, Georges, *On Nietzsche* (London: Continuum, 2004).

Blondel, Eric, *Nietzsche: The Body and Culture* (London: Athlone, 1991).

Derrida, Jacques, *Spurs: Nietzsche's Styles* (Chicago: University of Chicago Press, 1981).

Haar, Michel, *Nietzsche and Metaphysics* (New York: SUNY Press, 1996).

Heidegger, Martin, *Nietzsche*, 4 volumes (London: HarperCollins, 1991).

Jaspers, Karl, *Nietzsche: An Introduction to the Understanding of His Philosophical Activity* (Baltimore and London: Johns Hopkins University Press, 1997).

Kaufmann, Walter, *Nietzsche: Philosopher, Psychologist, Antichrist* (Princeton: Princeton University Press, 1975).

Klossowski, Pierre, *Nietzsche and the Vicious Circle* (London: Athlone, 1997).

Marsden, Jill, *After Nietzsche: Notes towards a Philosophy of Ecstasy* (Basingstoke: Palgrave Macmillan, 2002).

Nabais, Nuno, *Nietzsche and the Metaphysics of the Tragic* (London: Athlone, 2006).

ON *BEYOND GOOD AND EVIL*

Burnham, Douglas, *Reading Nietzsche: An Analysis of* Beyond Good and Evil (Stocksfield: Acumen, 2006).

Lampert, Laurence, *Nietzsche's Task: An Interpretation of* Beyond Good and Evil (Yale: Yale University Press, 2004).

ON THE *GENEALOGY OF MORALITY*

Davis Acampora, Christa (ed.), *Nietzsche's* On the Genealogy of Morals: *Critical Essays* (New York: Rowman & Littlefield, 2006).

Owen, David, *Nietzsche's* Genealogy of Morality (Stocksfield: Acumen, 2007).

ON HISTORY

Foucault, Michel, 'Nietzsche, Genealogy, History', in Paul Rabinow (ed.), *The Foucault Reader* (New York: Pantheon, 1984), pp. 76–100.

ON SCIENCE

Babich, Babette and Robert Cohen (eds), *Nietzsche, Epistemology, and Philosophy of Science*, 2 volumes (Dordrecht, Boston, London: Kluwer, 1999).

FURTHER READING

AND A NOVEL

Yalom, Irvin D., *When Nietzsche Wept* (New York: Perennial Classics, 2005).

INDEX